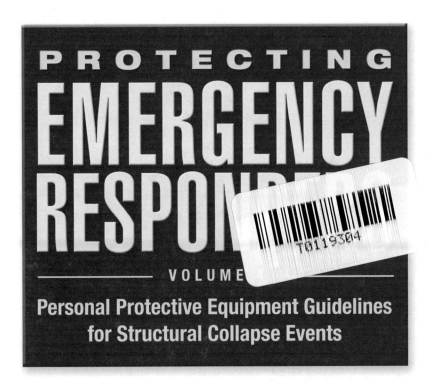

PROTECTING EMERGENCY RESPONDERS

VOLUME

Personal Protective Equipment Guidelines for Structural Collapse Events

Henry H. Willis, Nicholas G. Castle, Elizabeth M. Sloss, James T. Bartis

Prepared for the
National Institute for Occupational Safety and Health

 INFRASTRUCTURE, SAFETY, AND ENVIRONMENT

The research described in this report was a joint effort of the Science and Technology Policy Institute (operated by RAND from 1992-November 2003) and the National Institute for Occupational Safety and Health. This research was conducted under the auspices of the Safety and Justice Program within RAND Infrastructure, Safety, and Environment (ISE), a division of the RAND Corporation.

Library of Congress Cataloging-in-Publication Data is available for this publication.

ISBN: 0-8330-3907-5

The RAND Corporation is a nonprofit research organization providing objective analysis and effective solutions that address the challenges facing the public and private sectors around the world. RAND's publications do not necessarily reflect the opinions of its research clients and sponsors.

RAND® is a registered trademark.

Cover photo: Federal Emergency Management Agency

Published 2006 by the RAND Corporation
1776 Main Street, P.O. Box 2138, Santa Monica, CA 90407-2138
1200 South Hayes Street, Arlington, VA 22202-5050
201 North Craig Street, Suite 202, Pittsburgh, PA 15213-1516
RAND URL: http://www.rand.org/
To order RAND documents or to obtain additional information, contact
Distribution Services: Telephone: (310) 451-7002;
Fax: (310) 451-6915; Email: order@rand.org

Preface

Emergency workers who are likely to respond to a large structural collapse will encounter numerous physical, chemical, and biological hazards. This monograph provides guidelines for the use of personal protective equipment by emergency workers required to work in this environment. The emphasis of the monograph is on the first several days following a structural collapse, because it is during these initial days that the hazards are greatest, the response is most intense, site-specific exposure monitoring may not be available, and logistical challenges are greatest. These guidelines consider the full range of emergency workers who are likely to respond to a large structural collapse, including local fire, medical, and hazardous material teams as well as police officers and urban search and rescue teams.

The development of these guidelines was sponsored by the National Personal Protective Technology Laboratory of the National Institute for Occupational Safety and Health. A separate report, *Review of Literature Related to Exposures and Health Effects at Structural Collapse Events* (Sloss et al., 2005), reviews the possible health effects to emergency workers from exposure to conditions following a tall-building collapse.

The primary purpose of these publications is to serve as a technical source for incident commander guidelines that have been developed by NIOSH for broad distribution to the disaster management and emergency responder communities. In addition, these documents should be of interest to organizations responsible for developing equipment, standards, guidelines, and regulations for the protection of emergency responders.

This monograph is the fourth in a series of RAND publications, *Protecting Emergency Responders*. Other volumes in the series are the following:

- *Protecting Emergency Responders: Lessons Learned from Terrorist Attacks* (Jackson, Peterson et al., 2002)
- *Protecting Emergency Responders, Volume 2: Community Views of Safety and Health Risks and Personal Protection Needs* (LaTourrette et al., 2003)

- *Protecting Emergency Responders, Volume 3: Safety Management in Disaster and Terrorism Response* (Jackson, Baker et al., 2004).

The work leading to this monograph was begun under the auspices of the Science and Technology Policy Institute. The work was completed and published by RAND Infrastucture, Safety, and Environment.

The Science and Technology Policy Institute

Originally created by Congress in 1991 as the Critical Technologies Institute and renamed in 1998, the Science and Technology Policy Institute is a federally funded research and development center sponsored by the National Science Foundation. The Science and Technology Policy Institute was managed by the RAND Corporation from 1992 through November 30, 2003.

The Institute's mission has been to help improve public policy by conducting objective, independent research and analysis on policy issues that involve science and technology. To this end, the Institute performed the following functions:

- supported the Office of Science and Technology Policy and other Executive Branch agencies, offices, and councils
- helped science and technology decisionmakers understand the likely consequences of their decisions and choose among alternative policies
- helped improve understanding in both the public and private sectors of the ways in which science and technology can better serve national objectives.

In carrying out its mission, the Institute consulted broadly with representatives from private industry, institutions of higher education, and other nonprofit institutions.

The RAND Safety and Justice Program

This research was conducted under the auspices of the Safety and Justice Program within RAND Infrastructure, Safety, and Environment (ISE). The mission of RAND Infrastructure, Safety, and Environment is to improve the development, operation, use, and protection of society's essential physical assets and natural resources and to enhance the related social assets of safety and security of individuals in transit and in their workplaces and communities. Safety and Justice Program research addresses occupational safety, transportation safety, food safety, and public safety—including violence, policing, corrections, substance abuse, and public integrity.

Questions or comments about this monograph should be sent to the project leader, Henry Willis (Henry_Willis@rand.org). Information about the Safety and Justice Program is available online (www.rand.org/ise/safety). Inquiries about research projects should be sent to the following address:

Andrew Morral, Director
Safety and Justice Program, ISE
RAND Corporation
1200 South Hayes Street
Arlington, VA 22202-5050
703-413-1100 x5119
Andrew_Morral@rand.org

Contents

Figures

Tables

Summary

At the request of the National Institute for Occupational Safety and Health (NIOSH), the RAND Corporation undertook research and analyses to develop guidelines for personal protective equipment (PPE) for emergency responders to a large structural collapse. This work is motivated by the experiences of responders from the terrorist attacks on the Pentagon, the World Trade Center (WTC), and the Murrah Federal Building in Oklahoma City.

The primary purpose of this monograph is to serve as a technical source for incident commander guidelines that have been developed by NIOSH for broad distribution to the disaster management and emergency responder communities.

Scope and Approach

In this monograph, we characterize response activities and expected hazards, and develop guidelines for PPE following the collapse of a multistory commercial or residential building. We focus on the first days of response, because it is during this time that the hazards, uncertainty, response intensity, and logistical challenges are greatest. Precautions and PPE intended for chemical, biological, radiological, or nuclear attacks are not within the scope of our investigation.

During the first days following the collapse of a multistory building, responders and response managers rely on information that is readily available, such as visual cues or knowledge of the building's structural materials, contents, and occupants. The guidelines in this monograph translate this information into actionable steps responders can take in selecting, using, and maintaining PPE.

Hazards of Structural Collapse

The partial or complete collapse of a multistory building creates an array of physical, chemical, and biological hazards. The specific hazards present depend on the cause of the collapse (e.g., structural failure, earthquake, explosion), the magnitude of the failure (i.e., size of the building and completeness of the collapse), building materials and contents, the use and on-site storage of chemicals, the presence and duration of fires, and weather conditions during and immediately following the collapse.

These factors combine to create an environment containing multiple hazards. Physical hazards, from electrical equipment, noise, vehicles and heavy equipment, sharp objects, falling objects, and uneven or unsteady working surfaces, are a major cause of injuries and fatalities at building collapses. Chemical hazards can be created by fires and pulverization of building materials and contents. Biological hazards may exist, but situations in which they are substantial are easily characterized. Bloodborne pathogens, such as human immunodeficiency virus (HIV), the hepatitis B virus, and the hepatitis C virus, present risks only in the event of direct contact with infected bodily fluids. Such contact would occur only when responders are treating victims or handling human remains. Serious health consequences from other infectious diseases or waterborne pathogens are less likely and more easily managed. Significant sources of such hazards—pooled sewage, for instance—are easily identifiable.

Guidelines for PPE Ensembles at Multistory-Building Collapse Events

The guidelines focus on three issues that present unique challenges in the response to a multistory-building collapse: (1) protection from biological hazards; (2) protection from inhalation of hazardous materials; and (3) required modifications to responders' typical ensembles.

PPE Required for Protection from Biological Hazards

Biological hazards consist, primarily, of bloodborne and waterborne pathogens. Although potentially dangerous, detecting such hazards and protecting responders from them is straightforward.

Protection from Bloodborne Pathogens. Responders equipped with National Fire Protection Association (NFPA)–approved PPE generally do not require additional protection from bloodborne pathogens. Responders who are actively treating victims or working with human remains, however, must take extra precautions. These precautions include using gloves that provide resistance to viral pathogens (e.g., latex or nitrile gloves) and goggles or a faceshield to limit exposure to splashes of blood to the eyes, nose, and mouth. Since gloves designed to prevent the transmission of viruses are typically prone to puncture and tear, they must be used as undergloves (or replaced with more durable gloves) when moving through or handling rubble and debris.

Protection from Waterborne Pathogens. Infection from waterborne pathogens is only a concern if the pathogens are able to enter the body through cuts in the skin or contact with mucous membranes (i.e., the eyes, nose, or mouth). Exposures would result from contact with pools of sewage or contaminated water or from contact with waterborne pathogens in the dust at the collapse site. To protect against exposure from pools of sewage or contaminated water, water-resistant clothing and boots must be worn. When such equipment is not used, emergency responders must promptly remove contaminated equipment, wash exposed areas with soap and water, and acquire replacement or decontaminated PPE before resuming work. For protection from pathogens in dust, responders require a skin barrier that minimizes contact with the dust and provides protection from cuts, scrapes, and punctures.

PPE Required for Protection from Inhalation of Hazardous Materials
Environmental monitoring must be initiated as soon as possible. Obtaining complete and accurate information about the kind and level of chemical hazards that might be present in the air immediately following the collapse of a multistory building, however, will be difficult, if not impossible. Monitoring equipment will not be readily available, and other needs will be too pressing. Before data from direct monitoring are available, incident command must make on-the-spot decisions about what PPE must be worn to guard against present hazards. The use of visual cues and knowledge of building characteristics can aid this decisionmaking process.

If any of the following factors are present, all emergency responders in the area must wear respiratory protection: low oxygen levels, smoke from active and smoldering fires, irritant dusts (e.g., from concrete, glass, or other building materials), or chemical hazards (e.g., from silica, asbestos, metals, or organic compounds).

Protection in Oxygen-Deficient Environments. A supplied-air breathing apparatus, such as a self-contained breathing apparatus (SCBA), must be used in oxygen-deficient environments. If low-oxygen conditions are suspected or work is to be conducted in a confined space, oxygen levels in the air must be monitored. This can be done using the four-gas monitors typically used by firefighting companies.

Respiratory Protection Around Fires. When working around active fires, emergency responders should wear an SCBA for protection from carbon monoxide, organic compounds, and other hazardous byproducts of combustion. When working around fires is mission-critical, and supplied air respirators are either unavailable or their use is incompatible with the mission at hand, responders must use an air-purifying respirator (APR) and the work environment should be continuously monitored for oxygen and carbon monoxide levels.

A full-facepiece APR or powered air-purifying respirator (PAPR) with combined particulate, organic vapor, and acid gas cartridges may provide acceptable protection against the organic vapors and toxic gases present in smoke. However, APRs must not be worn for work in oxygen-deficient environments, as discussed previously, or in atmospheres that are immediately dangerous to life and health (IDLH), because failure of the mask or chemical cartridge would place a responder's life at risk. Incident commanders should be aware that, when exposure-monitoring data are not available, use of an APR can place responders at risk of hazardous exposure.

Respiratory Protection from Particulate Matter. When response activities require entry into areas where the visibility is less than 30 feet, responders must wear an SCBA. Half-mask APRs, full-facepiece APRs, and PAPRs are not appropriate at these high-particulate concentrations, because they will clog rapidly and will not provide adequate protection if responders encounter oxygen-deficient atmospheres or IDLH concentrations. Given the irritant nature of these dusts, individuals lacking respiratory protection who are exposed to these concentrations of dusts must be immediately removed from the site and provided with medical attention.

Even after the initial dust cloud has settled, work at the collapse site can resuspend hazardous quantities of dust. When visibility is greater than 30 feet and smoke plumes from active or smoldering fires are not present, visibility estimates suggest total dust concentrations will be less than 150 milligrams per cubic meter (mg/m^3). Under these conditions, either a PAPR or a full-facepiece APR with a combination particulate, organic vapor, and acid gas cartridge must be worn to provide adequate protection from dust. In high-dust conditions, a fabric prefilter must be used to prevent clogging of the cartridge. If eye protection is unnecessary or provided by goggles, a half-mask APR with the cartridge described previously and prefilter can be worn to provide adequate levels of protection. However, half-mask APRs will allow hazardous exposures when chemicals are present at concentrations above the calculated maximum-use concentration.

Given the large amount of dust generated at the WTC and Oklahoma City collapses, it is reasonable to expect that all responders to large structural collapse, even those serving in support roles, will need some respiratory protection. Thus, all responders should have access to at least half-mask APRs with combined particulate, organic vapor, and acid gas cartridges.

Protection from Chemical Hazards. Even when responders are protected from dusts and total particulates in the air, they may be exposed to hazardous chemicals that are constituents of these dusts. Asbestos and crystalline silica are of particular concern because of their toxicity and prevalence in building materials.

Monitoring data are required to select appropriate respirators properly. Without monitoring data, uncertainties in the magnitude and composition of respiratory exposures at a multistory-building collapse dictate that only SCBAs can ensure that responders are not exposed to hazardous chemicals at levels above NIOSH recommended exposure limits (RELs) or Occupational Safety and Health Administration (OSHA) permissible exposure limits (PELs). However, SCBAs are heavy and cumbersome, so using them can limit responders' abilities to engage in critical lifesaving tasks and may place them at even greater risk of immediate injury or death.

Using either PAPRs or APRs significantly decreases responder exposures. PAPRs provide several benefits over both APRs and SCBAs. Because PAPRs provide a constant supply of air at positive pressure using a battery-powered motor, they are not subject to the same fit testing requirements, mask fogging difficulties, and breathing hindrances that APRs present. In addition, they are lighter and less cumbersome than SCBAs. On the other hand, PAPRs are more expensive than APRs, require an adequate supply of recharged batteries, and consume more cartridge filters because air is constantly passed through them at a high rate.

Nevertheless, both PAPRs and APRs place responders at some level of marginal risk for the few days that they are responding at the collapse site. Although current knowledge of the chronic effects of short-term exposures does not provide a basis for quantifying this risk, it does suggest that these short-duration exposures present lower risks than lifetime exposures. In choosing between SCBAs, PAPRs, and APRs when exposure monitoring and assessment is not available, incident commanders must balance the increased burdens SCBAs present on lifesaving missions, risks SCBAs present for responders, and risks responders may face while using PAPRs and APRs.

PPE Ensemble Modifications

Immediately following a structural collapse, law enforcement, capable victims of the collapse, and witnesses near the incident generally become part of a spontaneous emergency response. None of these individuals will have the respiratory, head, eye, or skin protection against the hazards expected at a multistory-building collapse. Thus, all those involved in the immediate aftermath of the building collapse will require medical evaluation, and possibly medical attention and screening.

During the organized response, hazards from a multistory-building collapse will likely require additions or modifications to responders' standard PPE ensembles.

Urban Search and Rescue Ensembles. The urban search and rescue (USAR) ensemble, as specified in NFPA 1951 (NFPA, 2001a), is the most appropriate PPE ensemble for response to a multistory-building collapse. The exception occurs when fires or high temperatures are present, in which case a structural firefighting ensemble (NFPA 1971) (NFPA, 2000a) is required. Otherwise, the standard USAR ensemble requires three modifications needed to address the environment and hazards at a large structural collapse.

Additional Biological Protection. The USAR ensemble components are rated to provide an impermeable barrier from bloodborne pathogens; this barrier is only adequate so long as the gloves and their seams are intact. When exposure to bloodborne pathogens is more likely, USAR teams must wear further protection from biological hazards, such as latex or nitrile gloves and a faceshield.

Additional Respiratory Protection. USAR teams typically have access to no more than half-mask APRs. For work in the hot and warm zones, greater respiratory protection will likely be needed. USAR teams will need access to full-facepiece APRs, PAPRs, or SCBAs as necessary.

Excessively Heavy Helmets. The NFPA 1951 helmet standards currently provide more protection for heat than is needed when fires are not present. This additional thermal resistance makes the helmets heavy. In the absence of extreme heat conditions, the lighter NFPA 1977 (NFPA, 2005a) helmets are recommended.

Firefighter Ensembles. The ensemble for structural firefighting, as outlined in NFPA 1971, protects responders from severe hazards while they are working around active fires and intense heat. When fires are present, the NFPA 1971 ensemble must be worn. The greatest deficiency of the NFPA 1971 ensemble for response to a multistory-building collapse is that the heat protection incorporated into the NFPA 1971 makes its garments, gloves, and helmet heavy, cumbersome, and, depending on the weather, excessively warm. Wearing this ensemble places responders at risk of injury from falls or exhaustion. Thus, the NFPA 1971 ensemble should not be worn when excessive heat from fires is not a hazard.

In the absence of active fires, firefighters should wear the modified USAR ensemble discussed previously, which incorporates biological protection as necessary. Firefighters should also have access to respiratory protection other than SCBAs, such as full-facepiece APRs or PAPRs, and should be provided fit testing and training required for this equipment.

Emergency Medical Services Ensembles. The standard emergency medical services (EMS) PPE ensemble (NFPA 1999) (NFPA, 1992) is not intended to provide protection from many of the physical and chemical hazards expected from a multistory-building collapse. EMS personnel should wear clothing, gloves, footwear, and head protection equivalent to that worn by the USAR teams. Since EMS staff will most likely be treating victims, gloves and face protection from bloodborne hazards are still necessary. Finally, as with other emergency responders at the collapse site, EMS personnel must wear respiratory protection consistent with the standards specified previously.

Law Enforcement Ensembles. The primary roles of law enforcement during the initial hours and days of the response are to control the event perimeter and to investigate the site as a crime scene. For perimeter control, law enforcement responders should be removed from the physical and chemical hazards at the collapse unless assistance in access control is required in areas adjacent to those directly affected by the collapse event.

Additional PPE is necessary if law enforcement responders must enter areas of intense effort or support these efforts. In this event, law enforcement responders need head, eye, body, foot, hand, and respiratory equipment equivalent to the modified USAR ensemble discussed previously. Even if not entering these areas, all law enforcement officials will need viral penetration–resistant (e.g., latex or nitrile) gloves and eye and face protection if they are expected to assist in treating victims from the collapse.

PPE for Other Responders. If individuals from construction and trade industries, utility company personnel, or volunteers must work in and around the response effort, they must wear the modified USAR ensemble discussed previously along with all relevant occupation-specific PPE, such as eye protection for welders and insulating gloves for electrical workers. Since many of these individuals will not have access to the required PPE, emergency response planners must plan for the training and equipment supply necessary to protect these groups of responders.

Ensuring Availability and Appropriate Use of PPE

Selecting and purchasing appropriate PPE does not ensure safety; the equipment must also be readily available and must be used correctly. Thus, all emergency responders need to know where to get equipment, how to don it, what maintenance is required during use, when and how to clean or replace the PPE, and any limitations of the protective performance of the equipment.

Supply and Logistics

The typical PPE ensemble for some emergency responders will not be appropriate for use at a multistory-building collapse site. Also, additional equipment will be needed to replace and dispose of contaminated, damaged, or exhausted PPE. To address PPE supply and distribution problems, disaster management plans for metropolitan areas with multistory buildings should include logistical measures to disseminate rapidly and to maintain required PPE.

Integration and Compatibility

Incompatibilities between PPE components can compromise both the performance of the PPE and a responder's ability to work or maneuver. Thus, equipment must be tested to see how well various PPE components function together.

Training

Many responders at a multistory-building collapse will be using some types of PPE for the first time. Without proper training, responders can place themselves or others in harm's way. Since OSHA mandates training for the use of most PPE, especially respiratory protection, consideration must be given to either (1) how required training will be provided during disaster response or (2) how responders without proper training will be reassigned to appropriate tasks.

Decontamination

Decontamination of PPE and all body surfaces (e.g., skin and hair) must be conducted before any responder leaves the collapse site. The two primary sources of contamination in a post-structural collapse environment are (1) dust from fires and structural collapse, and (2) bloodborne pathogens from victims and human remains. Decontamination is required to ensure that emergency responders do not carry contamination with them off the site and, in doing so, endanger themselves and those around them.

Remaining Challenges for Protecting Emergency Responders at Multistory-Building Collapse Events

The most significant uncertainties are the composition and magnitude of the hazards present in the postcollapse environment. Although this uncertainty is reducible through hazard monitoring, this type of monitoring will not be available during the first few hours after a building collapse. Two areas that require further examination are the (1) logistical and practical demands of putting these protective guidelines into practice and (2) the uncertainties associated with the effects of infrequent, short-duration, multiple-chemical, high-magnitude exposures. These issues can only be addressed with investments in research to build a stronger understanding of the response community, technologies to improve PPE, and the health effects of hazardous exposures.

Acknowledgments

This research was conducted collaboratively with the National Personal Protective Technology Laboratory at the National Institute for Occupational Safety and Health. Jon Szalajda, Nadia El Ayouby, Roland BerryAnn, and John Dower provided extensive information and expertise in support of the research.

A panel of emergency responders was assembled to provide guidance to this research effort. Members of this panel, listed in the appendix, gave generously of their time, and their collective expertise was a valuable asset to the project.

The authors would also like to thank the members of the emergency responder community and federal agencies who generously contributed their time to this research effort. Participants from the Occupational Safety and Health Administration, the Federal Emergency Management Agency, the Centers for Disease Control and Prevention, the National Institute for Occupational Safety and Health, the National Institutes of Health, the National Institute of Environmental Health Sciences, and private industry are listed in the appendix.

Finally, the authors thank their RAND colleagues who shared ideas and gave generously of their time, including John Baker, Aarti Dalal, Jolene Galegher, Brian Jackson, Timothy LeDean, Jacqueline MacDonald, Merril Miceli, Amber Moreen, Stuart Olmsted, and Kenneth Shine.

Glossary

ACGIH	American Conference of Governmental Industrial Hygienists
AEGL	acute exposure guideline level
AIHA	American Industrial Hygiene Association
ANSI	American National Standards Institute
APF	assigned protection factor
APR	air-purifying respirator
ATSDR	Agency for Toxic Substances and Disease Registry
cc	cubic centimeter
CDC	Centers for Disease Control and Prevention
CFR	Code of Federal Regulations
dBA	A-weighted decibel
EEGL	emergency exposure guidance level
EMS	emergency medical services
EPA	Environmental Protection Agency
ERPG	emergency response planning guideline
FDNY	Fire Department of the City of New York
FEMA	Federal Emergency Management Agency
fibers/cc	fibers per cubic centimeter
hazmat	hazardous materials
HBV	hepatitis B virus
HCV	hepatitis C virus
HIV	human immunodeficiency virus
IDLH	immediately dangerous to life or health
kV	kilovolt

L	liter
μg	microgram
μg/m³	micrograms per cubic meter
μm	micrometer
m²/g	square meters per gram
mg/L	milligrams per liter
mg/m³	milligrams per cubic meter
n.d.	not detected
NFPA	National Fire Protection Association
ng/m³	nanograms per cubic meter
NIEHS	National Institute of Environmental Health Sciences
NIH	National Institutes of Health
NIOSH	National Institute for Occupational Safety and Health
NYPD	New York City Police Department
OSHA	Occupational Safety and Health Administration
PAH	polycyclic aromatic hydrocarbon
PAPR	powered air-purifying respirator
PCB	polychlorinated biphenyl
PEL	permissible exposure limit (OSHA)
PM	particulate matter
PMx	particulate matter of diameter less than x micrometers
PNOR	particulates not otherwise regulated
PPE	personal protective equipment
ppm	parts per million
REL	recommended exposure limit (NIOSH)
SCBA	self-contained breathing apparatus
STEL	short-term exposure limit
SVF	synthetic vitreous fiber
TEEL	temporary emergency exposure limit
TLV	threshold limit value
TPM	total particulate matter
TSCA	Toxic Substances Control Act
TWA	time-weighted average
USAR	urban search and rescue

USGS	United States Geological Survey
VOC	volatile organic compound
WEEL	workplace environmental exposure level
WTC	World Trade Center

CHAPTER ONE

Introduction

The unprecedented collapse of the World Trade Center (WTC) towers on September 11, 2001, has led to a number of initiatives to evaluate the preparedness of the United States to respond to future disasters. In particular, many in the emergency response community have expressed concern that the personnel who responded to the unfolding events at the WTC were not adequately outfitted with personal protective equipment (PPE) suitable for the long and strenuous rescue and recovery campaign. During the first days, quantitative monitoring data were not available to inform PPE selection. As the response continued, conflicting hazard assessments and directives for required PPE in the response zone added to emergency responders' confusion (Jackson, Peterson et al., 2002). Emergency responders' use of respirators at the WTC site was especially problematic. Even when respirators for protecting the emergency responders from the smoke, particles, and fumes were made available, clear guidelines were not provided for their selection or use. Consequently, the respirators were rarely worn, and hundreds of emergency responders today suffer from preventable injuries, including lung damage (CDC, 2002c).

Although multistory-building collapses have been infrequent, it is prudent for emergency response agencies in urban areas across the United States to make contingencies for hazards specific to these events. Almost every urban area has several multistory buildings. Furthermore, potential causes of building collapse—including earthquakes, natural gas explosions, hurricanes, engineering or construction failures, or terrorist actions—can occur anywhere across the United States.

Existing NIOSH guidelines provide recommendations for protecting emergency responders from the physical hazards of building collapse that may result while fighting structural fires (NIOSH, 1999). In contrast, this monograph establishes the foundation for the selection, use, and maintenance of PPE to protect responders from hazards that would exist following collapse of a multistory residential or commercial building. The monograph focuses on the first days of response following a multistory-building collapse. It is during these times that the hazards, uncertainty, response intensity, and logistical challenges are the greatest. Precautions and PPE intended for chemical, biological, radiological, or nuclear attacks are not within the scope of this analysis.

Project Approach

This research was performed by a multidisciplinary team consisting of RAND personnel and consultants with expertise in industrial hygiene, toxicology, epidemiology, chemistry, microbiology, exposure assessment, and emergency response. The study team also had access to NIOSH expertise in industrial hygiene and the performance and use of PPE.

During the first days of response to a multistory-building collapse, PPE selection and use guidelines must rely on information that will be readily available to responders. This requires relying largely on visual cues, such as detection of the presence of fires or certain hazardous chemicals. PPE selection and use can also pull from knowledge of the building's structural materials, contents, and occupants that can be maintained through periodic inspections. The guidelines in this monograph translate this type of information into actionable steps responders should take in selecting, using, and maintaining PPE during the incident.

These guidelines are the result of integration of knowledge from broad sources to inform emergency response planning:

- emergency response experiences with multistory-building collapse disasters and other disasters
- hazardous exposure monitoring and health effects literature
- experience of emergency response professionals.

Experience with Multistory-Building Collapses

The terrorist attacks on the WTC and the Pentagon and the bombing of the Murrah Federal Office Building in Oklahoma City were the primary sources for knowledge about hazardous exposures and challenges of emergency response to a multistory-building collapse event. A key source document for these lessons is the proceedings from a NIOSH/RAND working conference, "Protecting Emergency Responders: Lessons Learned from Terrorist Attacks" (Jackson, Peterson et al., 2002). Held in December 2001, this conference included individuals with firsthand experience in responding to the Pentagon, WTC, or Oklahoma City events. The proceedings captured the collective experiences from emergency responders to recent large terrorism events and provided the motivation for this monograph.

Hazardous Exposure Monitoring and Health Effects Literature

Though tragic, previous events do not provide a full representation of the range of possible hazards that should be expected at tall-building collapse events. Literature on exposure assessment, building and architectural materials, and chemical fate and transport provide insights into the range of hazards that could be present in a post–structural collapse environment and what the dominant routes of exposure may be. Studies of injuries and exposures at previous disasters, including the WTC collapse and the Oklahoma City bombing, document the prevalence of injuries and types of hazards at emergency response events. Finally, epidemiology and toxicology studies, particularly reviews by the Agency for Toxic Substances and Disease Registry (ATSDR), provide a scientific basis to inform PPE selection and use.

The goal of the literature review was to understand when selection or use of PPE in a post–structural collapse environment should depart from existing equipment standards and emergency response guidelines. Many organizations, including the National Fire Protection Association (NFPA), NIOSH, the Occupational Safety and Health Administration (OSHA), the Centers for Disease Control and Prevention (CDC), and the American National Standards Institute (ANSI), publish guidelines that form the foundation for this analysis.

Experience of Emergency Response Professionals

So that the guidelines reflect the constraints and realities of disaster response learned through experience, RAND established an advisory panel with expertise and practical experience in firefighting, law enforcement, urban search and rescue (USAR), and construction and trade support at disaster sites. This helped to ensure that the guidelines met the practical needs of the emergency response community. In addition, NIOSH invited other federal agencies and organizations representing the greater emergency response community to interact with RAND and its advisory panel during the course of the study. The appendix lists the members of the advisory panel and RAND-invited participants in the project review.

Structure of This Monograph

Chapter Two of this monograph provides details of lessons learned from the emergency response to the WTC tragedy, as relevant to developing guidelines for PPE needs at future multistory-building collapse events. Chapter Three characterizes the physical, chemical, and biological hazards that can be expected at a multistory-building collapse. Chapter Four provides an overview of important characteristics of the emergency response to a multistory-building collapse, including the organizations that will be involved, the types of PPE they conventionally use, the roles they will take on at the event, and how these activities will be organized spatially across the disaster site.

Building upon this foundation, Chapter Five provides guidelines for changes to emergency responders' PPE ensembles required because of hazards and activities specific to multistory-building collapse hazards and response. Chapter Six summarizes the guidelines for PPE use and maintenance throughout the first days of the response. Chapter Seven provides insights into additional equipment and planning needs that require further study.

CHAPTER TWO

The Need for PPE Guidelines: Learning from the WTC Tragedy

On September 11, 2001, two commercial aircraft were purposefully crashed into the World Trade Center towers. Each aircraft weighed approximately 200 tons and was traveling at about 470 miles per hour. The collisions fractured many of the perimeter support columns of the buildings, presumably weakening the structures. In each case, the aircraft's fuel supply ignited. The intense fire spread down the sides of the buildings, throughout the nearby floors and down interior elevator shafts to lower floors.

Almost immediately, the Fire Department of the City of New York (FDNY) and other emergency workers responded to the attacks and initiated rescue and recovery efforts. The fire in the buildings was estimated to be in excess of 2,000 degrees Fahrenheit (1,090 degrees Celsius), which exerted a large amount stress on the buildings' structural frames. The force of the collisions may have removed much of the fire-resistant material sprayed on the steel infrastructure, making it more susceptible to heat damage. Burning jet fuel ignited other materials within the buildings. The intense heat expanded and twisted the steel support structure causing it to buckle, gradually reducing the buildings' stability until they collapsed (Eager and Musso, 2001). Of the uniformed responders to the crashes, 343 FDNY firefighters, 23 New York City police officers, and 37 Port Authority officers died in the collapse (Hirschkorn, 2002), along with more than 2,000 civilians.

After the Collapse: The Response and the Hazards

Response to the collapse demanded New York City's full emergency response capacity, including FDNY, emergency medical services (EMS), and the New York City Police Department (NYPD). Within one hour, most FDNY units that were requested to dispatch to the WTC had done so, and within three hours, 200 units had responded—approximately half of FDNY's units (McKinsey, 2002b). Within one hour, 50 percent of all special operations units in the city were deployed (including hazardous materials [hazmat], rescue, high-rise, field communications, and tactical support). Approximately 100 ambulances responded within hours of the disaster. In the early stages of the response, the NYPD was involved with rescue activities and traffic control. Forty emergency service unit personnel, trained in collapses and hostage situations, responded to assist rescue efforts. Approximately 600 additional police officers controlled traffic around the site. Despite difficulties in estimating these efforts precisely, published counts of NYPD and FDNY responders at the WTC site on the first three days document the significance of the number of emergency responders involved (Table 2.1).

The resulting fires and debris at Ground Zero created an environment characterized by a diverse array of hazards including the following:

- rubble and debris
- rebar and steel trusses
- dust from pulverized glass, concrete, and asbestos
- hazardous metals and organic chemicals
- heat
- standing water
- power lines
- noise
- smoke from fires.

Table 2.1
Estimated NYPD and FDNY Response to the WTC Site

Personnel	Day 1	Day 2	Day 3
NYPD			
Rescue	600	700	700
Transportation	600	700	700
Site security	—	210	210
Investigation	—	—	—
FDNY			
Fire chief officers	27	25	25
Engine company personnel	600	600	600
Ladder company personnel	300	300	300
FDNY-EMS			
Supervisors	22	22	22
Municipal units	110	110	110
Voluntary units	84	84	84
Total	2,343	2,751	2,751

SOURCES: McKinsey (2002a, 2002b).

The magnitude and diversity of exposures at the collapse site severely hampered response activities. One emergency responder stated, "We found that atmospheric issues were so huge, you would have to back up to the river to get out of them. . . . You couldn't begin to move into an area safe from carbon monoxide, we couldn't find one" (Jackson, Peterson et al., 2002). The dust was also problematic. The U.S. Geological Survey (USGS) found pH levels of the dust to be highly corrosive (USGS, 2002). The mass of material deposited in the area was also high. Deposits of settled dust reached a thickness of more than 10 cm (Lioy and Gochfeld, 2002) at sites near the WTC. Seventy percent of this dust came from building materials such as pulverized cement.

Learning from the WTC Disaster

Responders to the WTC collapse faced a chaotic event and an uncertain array of hazards. Previous events and existing resources did little to prepare emergency responders for characterizing the hazardous exposures that could be present, or for selecting appropriate PPE. Several key lessons have emerged from examining the WTC collapse that should be incorporated into any future response to similar situations by emergency responders. These key lessons are as follows:

1. Respirator use is required to protect against airborne chemical and some biological hazards.
2. Clear answers are required to address confusion and concerns about biological hazards.
3. PPE must be compatible with the duration and intensity of the emergency response.
4. Advanced planning is required in response to logistical constraints on PPE availability.

Evidence of Respiratory Hazards

In a study of emergency workers with injuries and illnesses following the WTC collapse, the New York City Department of Health reviewed records from the emergency departments and inpatient admissions of four hospitals nearest the WTC and a fifth hospital with a burn referral center (CDC, 2002b). The New York City Department of Health team collected data from all persons seeking care at these facilities for the 48 hours following the collapse, beginning on September 11 and ending on September 13.

Within the first 48 hours, 279 rescue workers sought emergency care at the four hospitals near the WTC (CDC, 2002b). Of these, 118 (42 percent) had respiratory injuries, most of which were caused by exposure to smoke, dust, and fumes.

In a more detailed report of respiratory illness among rescue workers employed by the FDNY on September 11, 2001, the prevalence of respiratory illness was estimated among those with different exposures at the WTC site (Prezant et al., 2002). Patients were evaluated based on a questionnaire, spirometric testing, airway-responsiveness testing, and chest imaging. The main outcome, WTC cough, was defined as "a persistent cough that developed after exposure to the site and was accompanied by respiratory symptoms severe enough to require medical leave for at least four weeks" (Prezant et al., 2002, p. 806). Prezant et al. (2002) reported the incidence of WTC cough to be 8 percent among those present at the collapse of the WTC, 3 percent among those present within two days, 1 percent among those present within three to seven days, and 0 percent among those not at the WTC within the first two weeks (Table 2.2).

The incidence of respiratory illnesses requiring medical leave increased dramatically among FDNY rescue workers following the WTC attack (CDC, 2002a). The number of medical leaves due to respiratory illness was 1,876 in the 11 months following the attack, compared with 393 during the 11 months before the attack.

Fewer than half the workers at Ground Zero used respiratory protection (Lippy, 2002), but the evidence of the acute and chronic health effects from the event suggests that all workers in this area required some form of respiratory protection.

Table 2.2
Number and Percentage of Firefighters Employed by the FDNY on September 11, 2001, with WTC Cough, by Level of Exposure to Respiratory Irritants at the Site of the Collapse

Exposure Category	No. in Exposure Category	No. with WTC Cough	% with WTC Cough
High (present at WTC collapse)	1,636	128	7.8
Moderate (present within first two days after WTC collapse)	6,958	187	2.7
Low (present within three to seven days after WTC collapse)	1,320	17	1.3
None (not present first two weeks after collapse)	202	0	0.0
Total	10,116	332	3.3

SOURCE: Prezant et al. (2002).

Concerns About Biological Hazards

Emergency responders exhibited concern over the potential biological hazards at the WTC site (Jackson, Peterson et al., 2002). This is probably not surprising given that discussions of infectious agents are commonplace in the news media. Over the past several years, we have seen extensive news media coverage of human immunodeficiency virus (HIV), hepatitis, and Ebola virus, to name just a few examples.

Responder concerns arise in considering how to identify, avoid, and protect against biological hazards. Although the risk of infection may generally be small, the health consequences can sometimes be serious. Therefore, knowing where biological hazards exist, and how to protect responders from them, is an important part of emergency response planning and responder training.

Duration and Intensity of the Emergency Response

During the days after September 11, rescue operations continued 24 hours per day. Work shifts varied from 8 to 12 hours. In contrast, typical response activities for law enforcement, firefighters, and EMS personnel last less than a few hours in entirety. It is not surprising, then, that PPE selection and planning for multistory-building collapse events need to make special considerations for response duration and intensity.

Some PPE equipment, such as helmets or fire-protective clothing, can be very heavy. Some boots and respirators may cause discomfort or increased risk of heat stress because of prolonged use. These issues can lead to rapid fatigue or distractions, placing responders at greater risk in an already hazardous work environment. Comparing the standard components of responder PPE ensembles with the protection required at a multistory-building collapse event may identify opportunities to select PPE ensembles that are better suited for long, intense rescue and recovery campaigns.

Logistical Constraints on PPE Availability

As described previously, the response to the WTC disaster encompassed more than half of New York City's emergency response services. The preceding discussions suggest that PPE needed at a multistory-building collapse may differ from that used on a day-to-day basis. Responders can face serious respiratory hazards, uncertainty about biological hazards, and must perform this work as part of an intense and continuous response during the days following the collapse. Supplying, using, and maintaining appropriate PPE require that all emergency responders likely to be involved in rescue operations after a structural collapse have access to proper equipment and receive all training and testing required for effective PPE use and maintenance. The WTC events revealed that supplying required equipment and training proves challenging, and that the process would benefit if these factors were accounted for in emergency response planning in areas with multistory buildings.

This logistics challenge is also relevant for hazard monitoring and assessment. These functions are particularly important because they provide the definitive means for selective PPE. The sooner PPE selection is based upon measured hazards, as opposed to the guidelines developed in this monograph, the sooner emergency responders will be assured of fully adequate and effective protection. The WTC incident demonstrated challenges of hazard monitoring and assessment immediately after a large-scale disaster.

CHAPTER THREE

Characterization of Post–Structural Collapse Hazards

Partial or complete collapse of a multistory building creates an environment characterized by a diverse array of hazards. The specific hazards present will be determined by the cause of the collapse (e.g., structural failure, earthquake, explosion), the magnitude of the failure (i.e., size of the building and completeness of the collapse), building contents and materials, building use and on-site chemical storage, and weather conditions during and immediately following the collapse. These factors combine to create a mix of physical, chemical, and biological hazards in the post-collapse environment. While the hazards at any given collapse will depend on specific circumstances of the structure and its collapse, this chapter describes the range of hazards that might be expected across all types of events.

Little monitoring data are available about hazardous exposures during the first few days at large post–structural collapse events. Thus, the hazard characterizations presented in this chapter are based on reviews of responder injury and fatality data at disasters, literature on materials used for building structural and mechanical systems, available data from the WTC collapses, and monitoring data from municipal fire events.

This exposure information forms the basis for anticipating what the PPE needs of emergency responders may be at future collapse events. This analysis approach is specifically intended to provide foresight about potential exposures to support emergency response planning, equipment acquisition, and training efforts related to building collapse events.

Physical Hazards

Rescue work at a building collapse can be extremely demanding physically. Self-evident physical hazards at any emergency response include unstable work surfaces, falling objects or collapsing structures, working around heavy equipment and vehicles, and the physiological effects of working intensely for a long duration in very hot (or very cold) weather. In addition to these common physical hazards, a multistory-building collapse event presents several hazards that are unique in nature. Key aspects of electrical hazards, fires and explosions, excessive noise, and asphyxiation hazards are discussed below.

Downed and Severed Electrical Wires or Cables

Downed and severed electrical cables often run through the rubble of collapsed and partially collapsed buildings. If power supplies to the entire site have not been disconnected, these cables present a potentially fatal electrocution risk. Emergency responders can also suffer injury from nonfatal electric shock, cardiac arrhythmias, electric burns, or falls following electric shock (NIOSH, 1998b).

Injuries from electricity can occur from direct contact with the electric source, arcing of electricity through the air to the emergency responder, or thermal burns from the heat generated by the electricity or ignition of clothing. Direct injury by electric current depends on the amperage, region of the body affected, penetration of the electric current, and duration of electrical exposure (NIOSH, 1998b).

Structural collapse could affect building, distribution, and transmission power lines. For very tall buildings, local distribution voltages—between 7 and 14 kilovolts (kV)—may be present throughout the structure, and power may be delivered to the building at transmission voltages—typically between 66 and 230 kV (NIOSH, 1998b; Makens, 1996).

In the course of a multistory-building collapse, there is likely to be water exposure to emergency responders from water main breaks, sprinkler systems, or firefighting activities. This water exposure increases the risks of electrical hazards.

Fire and Explosion

Building collapse can be caused by or can lead to fires and explosions at the collapse site. Building materials, building contents, on-site fuel storage, and natural-gas pipelines can provide fuel for fires and explosions. In the case of terrorism events, bombs or sabotage of storage areas for flammable chemicals may initiate fires and explosions. For other causes of structural failure, heating systems, severed electrical lines, or punctured pressure vessels can lead to fire or explosions. In addition to burn and smoke inhalation injuries, fire and explosions increase risks from falling objects and collapsing structures. The presence of flammable materials in collapsed or partially collapsed structures puts emergency responders at risk from exposure to secondary explosions and their effects.

Excessive Noise

Firefighters and emergency medical technicians tend to have accelerated levels of hearing loss (Tubbs, 1995). Short-term exposure to high noise levels can cause temporary hearing loss; prolonged exposure to high noise levels can lead to permanent hearing loss. While hearing loss usually occurs over time and not generally from a single incident, an intense noise can cause hearing damage much more quickly.

Occupational noise exposure is measured using A-weighted decibels (dBA), a logarithmic scale adjusted to the frequencies detected by the human ear. Intense, explosive noise in the range of 140–160 dBA can cause acute acoustic trauma to the ear, resulting in hearing loss and tinnitus (Axelson and Hamernick, 1987). Tympanic membrane rupture occurs in about a third of acute acoustic trauma exposures (Rom, 1998). These exposures also can cause ossicle bone disruption, oval window damage, and cochlear hair cell disruption (Hanner and Axelsson, 1988; Ylikoski, 1989).

Operations at building collapse sites are inherently noisy. Excavating equipment, cutting and drilling tools, and emergency vehicles generate noise at levels that can cause temporary or permanent hearing damage. For example, median dBA measurements for bulldozers, jackhammers, and air compressors have been recorded at 89, 104, and 96 dBA, respectively (Suter, 2002).

To put these noise measurements in perspective, NIOSH recommends that occupational exposure be controlled to less than 85 dBA as a time-weighted average (TWA), with exposure duration halved as noise levels increase by 3 dBA (see Table 3.1). NIOSH guidance states further that peak noise exposures should not exceed 140 dBA. Workers exposed to noise levels in excess of NIOSH guidelines may suffer permanent noise-induced hearing loss (NIOSH, 1998a).

A limited body of literature suggests that some chemicals may aggravate the rate of hearing loss. At a building collapse site, emergency responders may be exposed to several of these ototoxic chemicals. For example, structure fires produce cyanide and carbon monoxide, both of which may increase hearing loss. However, the findings of this literature remain preliminary and do not provide much in the way of permissible exposure levels; thus, there is little to support recommendations to control exposure based on potential ototoxic effects (Fechter, Chen, and Johnson, 2002; Fechter, Young, and Carlisle, 1988; Levine and Radford, 1978; Morata, Dunn, and Sieber, 1994; Radford and Levine, 1976; Treitman, Burgess, and Gold, 1980).

Table 3.1
NIOSH Standards for Hearing Protection

Permissible Exposure Duration (Per Day)	Time-Weighted Average Exposure Magnitude (dBA)
8 hours	85
4 hours	88
2 hours	91
1 hour	94
30 minutes	97
15 minutes	100
7 minutes	103

SOURCE: NIOSH (1998a).

Asphyxiation Hazards

Normal atmospheres contain approximately 21 percent oxygen, 78 percent nitrogen, and small amounts of other gases. Low oxygen conditions can result when the oxygen in air is consumed or displaced. Oxygen consumption can occur when combustion occurs in a poorly ventilated area or when a large number of people work in a confined space. Displacement of oxygen can occur when large amounts of gases are released into confined areas or when gases with vapor densities greater than oxygen accumulate in poorly ventilated depressions. Sources of gas releases can include damage to storage tanks or exhaust from vehicles or machinery. Examples of gases that may accumulate in poorly ventilated spaces include Freon®[1] (used as a refrigerant) and carbon dioxide (used in fire-suppression systems). The combination of fires, chemical releases, vehicles, and confined areas or enclosed areas creates asphyxiation hazards following a building collapse.

Health effects from oxygen deficient environments are not evident until oxygen concentrations fall below 17 percent. The first signs of oxygen deprivation include deteriorated night vision, heavier breathing, and increased heart rate. When oxygen concentrations fall to between 14 percent and 16 percent, muscle coordination degrades, individuals become rapidly fatigued, and breathing patterns may become heavy and intermittent. Concentrations of oxygen between 6 percent and 10 percent lead to nausea, vomiting, an inability to perform tasks, and eventually loss of consciousness. Atmospheres with less than 6 percent oxygen are extremely dangerous, with exposure leading to spasmatic breathing, convulsive movements, and death after only a few minutes of exposure (OSHA, undated).

Chemical Hazards

The only means for definitely characterizing chemical hazards is through exposure monitoring and assessment. Thus, exposure monitoring should be initiated as soon as possible during emergency response. However, there will always be periods before exposure monitoring is available. To inform PPE selection under these circumstances, this section provides an overview of the chemical hazards that might be expected at a multistory-building collapse.

As buildings collapse, construction materials can become pulverized, creating a cloud of respirable dust particles that can linger from hours to days. Building collapse can damage chemical storage tanks and containers, releasing clouds of hazardous gases. Fires, which may either have caused the building collapse or have been initiated by it, add to the mix of chemicals in the air around the collapse site. Incomplete

---

[1] Freon® is a registered trademark of DuPont.

combustion creates a complex mixture of compounds from chemicals present in building materials or building contents.

Chemicals stored in significant quantities in residential or commercial structures are typically limited to pressurized gases and fuel oils. For example, air conditioning systems contain large amounts of compressed gases as refrigerants (e.g., Freon or ammonia) and some fire-suppression systems use compressed carbon dioxide. Liquid storage in multistory buildings is generally limited to day tanks for chemical storage (e.g., diesel for backup power, water treatment chemicals for scale control or biological inhibition in boilers, or cleaning solutions) and water to maintain building supplies for drinking and fire control. Because these chemicals will be present in small quantities, their concentrations will be diluted in the debris of a building collapse. Some multistory buildings use oil-fired boilers for heat and hot water, and store large amounts of oil. No significant storage of powders or solid chemicals is expected at a typical large commercial or residential building.

Common tenants of large commercial buildings may use other hazardous materials. For example, swimming pool systems incorporate storage of liquid chlorine chemicals, and dry-cleaning facilities use chlorinated organic compounds such as perchloroethylene. Similarly, outpatient medical facilities, such as medical and dental offices, may store pharmaceuticals, laboratory chemicals, and medical waste. The quantities of these chemicals will generally be small compared with the total amount of dust and debris generated during a multistory-building collapse. Thus, the hazard characterization presented in this section assumes that tenant operations are not significant sources of chemical hazards. However, information from periodic building inspections should be used to help inform responders of the chemical hazards they may face in any specific collapse.

The magnitude of risk resulting from chemicals in building materials will be mediated by two criteria:

1. *Demonstrated toxicity:* While most chemicals are toxic at sufficient dose, potency of irritants, toxicants, and carcinogens can vary by orders of magnitude. Furthermore, severity and immediacy of effects can also vary widely.
2. *Prevelance in buildings or building materials:* A chemical is not likely to create a hazardous exposure if it is not present in buildings in large enough quantities. The more common its uses are in buildings, the greater the potential for hazardous exposure at a building collapse site.

Both of these factors (toxicity and prevalence) must be considered when assessing hazard at a building collapse.

Forms of Chemical Hazards

Most chemical hazards at a multistory-building collapse are present as coarse dusts, aerosol, or gases (visible or invisible). Aerosols are dispersions of solid or liquid particles in air that are slow to settle by gravity. Depending on their particle size and physical states, aerosols can be classified as mists, smog, fumes, fine dusts, or sprays (see Figure 3.1). Aerosols range from approximately 0.01 micrometer (μm) to 20 μm in diameter.[2] Inhalation exposures to aerosols depend on how deeply they can travel into the respiratory system (World Health Organization, 1999). The *inhalable* fraction of aerosols consists primarily of particles smaller than 10 μm. Most particles between 3.5 μm and 4.0 μm, the *thoracic* fraction, are small enough to enter the lungs but too large to reach gas-exchange regions. Particles smaller than 3.5 μm, the *respirable* fraction, can enter deep into the lung where gas exchange occurs (ACGIH, 2003). Inhalable particulates are typically measured as PM10 (all particles less than 10 μm in diameter) and PM2.5 (less than 2.5 μm in diameter). As this nomenclature implies, smaller particles penetrate more deeply into the respiratory system and generally result in exposures that are more hazardous.

Figure 3.1
Particle Size and Classification

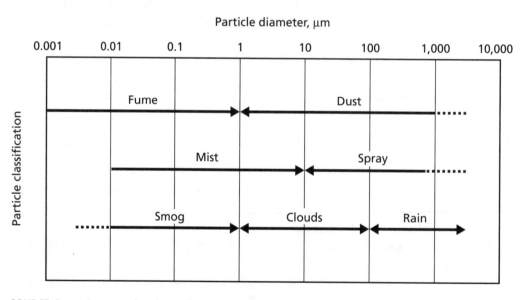

SOURCE: Perry, Green, and Maloney (1984).
RAND *MG425-3.1*

---

[2] Particulates smaller than 0.01 μm are classified as large molecules, and those larger than 20 μm settle quickly by gravity (Perry, Green, and Maloney, 1984).

Exposures from hazardous gases would typically result from fires, vehicle exhaust, or damage to a gas-storage container or natural-gas pipeline. Some gases, such as chlorine, can form visible clouds. As concentrations of these clouds decrease, through dilution or dispersion, they may become invisible but remain hazardous. Though not visible, presence of many colorless gases (e.g., sulfur dioxide, ammonia, or natural gas doped with mercaptans) can be detected by smell. Although these smells provide warning of dangerous gas, rapid onset of olfactory fatigue limits detection by smell of some gases. Colorless gases are particularly hazardous when they are also odorless, like carbon dioxide or Freon.

Composition of Chemical Hazards

The materials used for building construction and on-site storage will largely determine chemicals present at a building collapse. Chemicals present at a building collapse are produced either by pulverization of building materials during the collapse or as byproducts of combustion.

The two main materials in the skeletal frameworks of U.S. buildings are concrete and steel. In addition, the use of glass in high-rise facades surged in the 1960s (Ford, 1992). The building's primary use and height lend clues as to what materials were likely to have been used in its construction. Taller buildings tend to be used for commercial or mixed use and are supported by steel or composite systems (i.e., skeletal systems in which both steel and concrete are used together such that neither material predominates over the other). Residential buildings tend to be shorter and supported by concrete. Although steel is still common for office and commercial buildings today, most residential towers are built with concrete (Ford, 1992).

Structural materials may not, however, be the most potent hazardous materials in a building. Materials used in smaller quantities for special purposes can create important hazards for emergency responders. As discussed below, polychlorinated biphenyls (PCBs) and asbestos are examples of such substances.

Chemicals present in the collapse environment can be categorized into five groups based on chemical composition and properties:

1. particulate matter
2. metals
3. chlorinated hydrocarbons
4. volatile organic compounds (VOCs)
5. polycyclic aromatic hydrocarbons (PAHs).

The following sections address the toxicity and sources (or uses) of specific compounds in each of the five groups of chemicals listed above. Sloss et al. (2005) provide detailed reviews of the health effects for selected examples of chemicals in each of these groups.

Particulate Matter. Exposure to particulate matter (PM) can result from the initial dust cloud following a building collapse, fires at the site, and resuspension of dust by emergency responders working at the collapse site. The bulk of particulate matter generated at a building collapse will result from the building's structural and architectural materials, including concrete (see Table 3.2). In forming, particles may adsorb organics, metals, and metal oxides resulting from pulverization or fires. The result will be a possibly highly alkaline, multiple-component mix of aerosols.

Total particulate matter can have effects on both human mortality (Dockery et al., 1993; Samet et al., 2000) and morbidity (Abbey et al., 1998) following brief exposures. Moderate exposures to particulate matter (i.e., tens to hundreds of micrograms per cubic meter [$\mu g/m^3$]) have been associated with increased mortality among individuals with compromised cardiovascular function (Dockery et al., 1993; Samet et al., 2000). Morbidity following exposure to high levels of particulate matter includes exacerbation of asthma and lung irritation (Abbey et al., 1998). Specific constituents of particulate matter listed in Table 3.2, such as asbestos, synthetic vitreous fibers, and silica, present additional human health concerns.

Detailed summaries of the health effects literature for particulate matter and these specific constituents are included in Sloss et al. (2005).

Table 3.2
Building and Architectural Materials That Constitute Particulate Matter from a Multistory-Building Collapse

Material or Chemical Class	Use in Building Materials
Asbestos	Insulation, concrete reinforcement, and fire retardant and fireproofing materials
Calcite	Cement, wall boards, fiberglass, and glass
Calcium Chloride	Concrete additive
Dolomite	Cement, glass, fiberglass, and plastic and paint additive
Gypsum	Cement, plaster, and wall board
Halite	Water-softening agent and plastic additive
Isocyanates	Binders and foam
Kaolin	Floor and wall tiles
Mica	Concrete additive
Portlandite	Cement
Silica	Glass, cement, bricks, rubber additive, insulation, paints, coatings, and adhesives
Synthetic vitreous fibers	Insulation (e.g., fiberglass)

SOURCES: Berge and Henley (2000), Hornbostel (1991), USGS (2001).

Inhalation of asbestos fibers may cause lung cancer and mesothelioma. Asbestos was widely used as a concrete additive, insulation material, and fire retardant. In addition, asbestos was used as an additive to asphalt, vinyl materials in roof shingles and coatings, pipes, siding, wall board, floor tiles, building panels, joint compounds, adhesives, acoustical plaster, electrical insulating materials, and mixtures sprayed on ceilings and walls. The National Emission Standards for Hazardous Air Pollutants banned asbestos for fireproofing or insulating in 1973. This included most spray-applied applications of asbestos to structural systems. The Environmental Protection Agency (EPA) also banned the use of asbestos for wet-applied and preformed asbestos pipe insulation (1975), preformed asbestos block insulation on boilers and hot-water tanks (1975), and uses for "decorative purposes" (1978). In 1993, the Toxic Substances Control Act (TSCA) banned additional asbestos-containing products, including corrugated paper, roll board, commercial and specialty paper, flooring felt, and any new uses of asbestos (EPA, 1999). Collapses involving buildings built after the 1980s are less likely to involve significant exposures to asbestos.

Synthetic vitreous fibers (SVFs) are fibrous, inorganic materials that are primarily used as insulation. There are three categories of SVFs: (1) glass fibers (fiberglass), including glass wool and continuous-filament glass; (2) mineral wool, which contains stone wool and slag wool; and (3) refractory ceramic fibers (ATSDR, 2004). SVFs may provide a large source of particulate matter in cases of full or extensive building collapse. Studies at the WTC collapse indicate that fibers were a major component of dusts created by the WTC collapses. Fibers were primarily glass (i.e., amorphous silica), cellulose (i.e., from paper), and mineral fibers from insulation (Lioy et al., 2002). Health effects of SVFs range from respiratory irritation or pulmonary inflammation to pulmonary fibrosis and possibly lung cancer.

The term *silica* refers to the chemical compound silicon dioxide, which occurs in crystalline and noncrystalline (amorphous) forms. Amorphous silica is used in many products, including glass, fillers in the rubber industry, paints, silicon rubber, insulation material, coatings, and adhesives. Crystalline silica is believed to be more hazardous than amorphous silica, and its most common form is quartz. In this form, crystalline silica is used in many building materials, including bricks, architectural rocks, and cement. Health effects of silica include acute and chronic silicosis, pulmonary tuberculosis, chronic bronchitis, chronic obstructive pulmonary disease, lung cancer, and possibly autoimmune diseases.

Metals. Beyond structural applications, metals are used for pigments, piping, electrical devices, electronic components, lamps, architectural alloys, and wood preservatives. Table 3.3 provides a listing of common hazardous metals used in buildings. Ingestion, inhalation, or dermal contact may lead to hazardous exposure, although inhalation is the most important route for dust and particulate-type exposures generated at a structural collapse. Health effects of heavy metals include acute toxic reactions, such as irritation of the upper and lower respiratory systems, cancer, and organ damage from chronic exposure. Sloss et al. (2005) provide health-effects reviews for arsenic, cadmium, chromium, lead, and mercury. These metals were selected based on the combination of toxicity and prevalence in building materials.

Table 3.3
Hazardous Metals Found in Building and Architectural Materials

Material or Chemical Class	Use in Building Materials
Aluminum	Structural metals, metal fixtures, and interior components
Arsenic	Impregnated timber, pigments, and alloys
Barite	Pigments
Beryllium	Electrical components and steel additive
Boric salts	Impregnated timber, fire retardant, and plastic additive
Cadmium	Pigments, plastic additive, and steel additive
Chromium	Pigments, impregnated timber, and steel additive
Cobalt	Pigments and steel additive
Copper	Pipe, wire, roofing, impregnated timber, and pigments
Iron	Steel and pigments
Lead	Pigments, concrete additive, pipe, solder, and plastic additive
Magnesium	Cement, brick, insulation, alloys, and glass
Manganese	Pigments, steel, and other alloys
Mercury	Pigments, lamps, and electrical devices
Molybdenum	Steel
Nickel	Steel, stainless steel, alloys, and pigments
Selenium	Glass, alloys, and pigments
Silver	Electrical components
Tellurium	Steel and alloys
Titanium	Pigments and alloys
Vanadium	Steel
Zinc	Steel, alloys, pigments, and textile and wood preservatives

SOURCES: Berge and Henley (2000), Hornbostel (1991), USGS (2001).

Chlorinated Hydrocarbons. Chlorinated hydrocarbons that might be present at a building collapse include dioxins, vinyl chloride, halogen-based refrigerants (e.g., Freon) and PCBs. The most common source of most chlorinated hydrocarbons at a building collapse will be combustion byproducts. Other sources include the use of chlorinated hydrocarbons in building materials such as plastics, synthetic textiles, insulation materials, adhesives, and coatings. Freon and PCBs are used in building maintenance systems. Health effects of chlorinated hydrocarbons include acute toxicity, cancer, and organ damage. The use of Freon®12[3] has been discontinued in the United States because of its effects on the earth's ozone layer. However, other Freon compounds are still commonly used in building air conditioning systems. While these new hydrocarbon refrigerants are less damaging to the ozone layer, they still pose serious health hazards. PCBs were used as coolants in transformers before being banned for this use in 1977. However, PCB-containing transformers may still be in use in older buildings (ATSDR, 2001).

Sloss et al. (2005) provide health-effects reviews of dioxins and PCBs. These chemicals were selected based on their toxicity and likely presence in the post–structural collapse environment.

Volatile Organic Compounds. The largest source of VOCs at a building collapse will most likely be from incomplete combustion of organic materials. VOCs are organic chemicals with high vapor pressures. This property causes these liquids to evaporate readily. Examples of VOCs associated with building materials include benzene, ethylbenzene, styrene, toluene, and xylene. Common uses include adhesives, paints, coatings, and the manufacture of plastics and organic textiles. Hazardous exposures may occur through dermal, inhalation, or ingestion routes. The health effects of VOCs include acute toxic reactions and cancer or permanent organ damage from chronic exposure.

Sloss et al. (2005) provide a health-effects review of benzene. Benzene was selected because it is a common by-product of combustion of organic materials and therefore would be expected in the postcollapse environment.

Polycyclic Aromatic Hydrocarbons. PAHs, some of which are classified as known or suspected human carcinogens, are organic chemicals that have a chemical structure comprising multiple benzene rings. Examples of PAHs include anthracene, benzo(a)anthracene, benzo(a)pyrene, benzo(b)fluoranthene, chrysene, phenanthrene, and pyrene. PAHs are typically not readily biodegradable or soluble in water—properties that make them well suited for waterproofing. PAHs are also common by-products from the incomplete combustion of organic materials.

---

[3] Freon®12 is a registered trademark of DuPont.

Sloss et al. (2005) provide a health-effects review of PAHs. PAHs were selected because they are common by-products of incomplete combustion, and therefore would be expected in the postcollapse environment.

Magnitude of Exposures at a Collapse Site

Data on exposures to hazardous substances from building collapse events are sparse. The most relevant source of data is exposure monitoring from the WTC tragedies. These data are limited by the fact that most data were not collected until several days after the towers had collapsed. However, they provide a basis for suggestion of what materials may have been present at hazardous concentrations during the early hours and days of the response.

Studies on firefighter exposures from municipal fires also provide indication of exposures that might be present. These data are relevant because fires were a significant source of exposure at the WTC and are likely to be present at other multistory-building collapses.

Documented Exposures at the World Trade Center Collapse. The EPA collected the most extensive environmental monitoring data from the WTC site. However, no data from the EPA are available prior to September 14. OSHA and NIOSH also reported air monitoring in published studies, but this data collection did not begin until September 13 for OSHA and September 18 for NIOSH.

Comprehensive air sampling was not immediate due to several problems, including the limited number of portable sampling machines, limited accessibility to the collapse site, and lack of electricity (Lioy and Gochfeld, 2002).

These monitoring results suggest that many chemical exposures were above normal ambient levels. A more limited set of exposures was at or just above NIOSH recommended exposure limits (RELs) or OSHA permissible exposure limits (PELs). These elevated levels are significant because they were not measured when exposures were at their greatest. By the time these measurements were taken, the tremendous dust clouds created by the initial collapse had settled, much of the dust had been widely dispersed by winds, fires on the site were less intense, and rain a few days after the collapse had further reduced exposures. This suggests that much higher exposures of these chemicals may have been present during the first hours and days following the WTC collapses. Some results of these monitoring studies are summarized below.

Asbestos. OSHA and NIOSH presented results of 1,425 and 804 asbestos air samples, respectively (NIOSH, 2002; OSHA, 2002). OSHA sampling began on September 13, 2001, around lower Manhattan and continued for several months around the collapse site. NIOSH sampling was conducted from September 18 through October 4 in the collapse site and areas immediately adjacent to the debris pile. Most of these results were below the NIOSH REL and OSHA PEL of 0.1 fibers per cubic centimeter (fibers/cc) (55 percent of the NIOSH samples and 88 percent of the OSHA samples were below these exposure limits). However, NIOSH reported concentrations as high as 0.89 fibers/cc, indicating that some exposures were above regulated exposure limits and suggesting that levels may have been even higher during the first hours following the WTC collapses.

Volatile Organic Compounds. NIOSH reported results from 76 air samples collected around Ground Zero that were monitored between September 18 and October 4 for VOCs, including benzene, ethylbenzene, styrene, toluene, and xylene (NIOSH, 2002). Only trace amounts of chemicals were detected in most of these samples. However, two benzene samples (0.35 mg/m³ and 0.46 mg/m³) exceeded the NIOSH REL of 0.32 mg/m³ but not the OSHA PEL of 3.2 mg/m³. OSHA reports of 707 samples for VOCs suggest that elevated levels (on the order of OSHA PELs) were largely confined to areas around the plumes from burning fires (OSHA, 2002).

Dioxins. Between September and November 2001, EPA measured dioxin concentrations around Ground Zero ranging from 10 picograms toxic equivalents per cubic meter to more than 150 picograms toxic equivalents per cubic meter (National Center for Environmental Assessment, 2002; EPA, 2002). These results suggest that fires at the WTC elevated dioxin levels above typical ambient concentrations of 0.1–0.2 picograms toxic equivalents per cubic meter. OSHA sampling supports EPA findings, with 1 of 10 samples having shown dioxin levels above background levels (OSHA, 2002). Neither OSHA nor NIOSH has set TWAs or short-term exposure limits for dioxins. However, dioxins have been classified as known human carcinogens by two health agencies.

Metals. OSHA and NIOSH monitored for dust, oxides, and fumes of metals such as antimony, arsenic, beryllium, cadmium, chromium, cobalt, copper, iron, lead, magnesium, manganese, mercury, molybdenum, nickel, vanadium, and zinc. These results indicate that metal concentrations were generally below OSHA PELs. EPA air monitoring results indicate similar levels of metals in air samples tested. However, OSHA and NIOSH reported overexposures of copper, iron oxide, lead, zinc oxide, and cadmium for workers engaged in torch cutting and burning (NIOSH, 2002; OSHA, 2002).

Particulate Matter. Particles less than 2.5 micrometers in diameter (PM2.5) are defined as fine particulate matter. These particles include smoke and dust. The highest concentrations of PM2.5 detected by EPA monitoring were on the order of 200 μg/m³ (National Center for Environmental Assessment, 2002). Though above EPA's 24-hour air quality index of 40 μg/m³, these peak concentrations are significantly below the OSHA PEL for respirable particulates of 5 mg/m³. NIOSH sampling of respirable particulates confirm EPA findings, indicating that the maximum detected concentration of PM2.5 was 0.32 mg/m³ (NIOSH, 2002).

Both OSHA and NIOSH also analyzed air samples for respirable silica. NIOSH results did not detect silica in any air samples collected at and around the collapse site between September 18 and October 4. However, OSHA detected silica levels above

Figure 3.2
The Dust Cloud of Tower One, September 11, 2001

SOURCE: David Thom (2001).
RAND *MG425-3.2*

the OSHA PEL in 94 exposure samples. These samples were collected at the WTC in work areas with jack hammering, drilling, loading rubble, and breaking or chipping concrete (NIOSH, 2002; OSHA, 2002).

It is important to point out that the EPA specifically notes that personal accounts and photographs on September 11 suggest that particulate concentrations could have been as high as hundreds of milligrams per cubic meter (mg/m³) (National Center for Environmental Assessment, 2002). Photos (see Figure 3.2) and anecdotal reports of visibility following the towers' collapse support this conclusion.

Polychlorinated Biphenyls. The highest concentration of PCBs measured by EPA air monitoring was 153 nanograms per cubic meter (ng/m³) on October 2, 2001. This observed level is significantly below the NIOSH REL of 1,000 ng/m³ and the OSHA PEL of 5,000 ng/m³ (National Center for Environmental Assessment, 2002). OSHA and NIOSH did not report data on PCB exposures.

Polycyclic Aromatic Hydrocarbons. Four of 12 NIOSH samples for PAHs detected trace amounts of PAHs that are human carcinogens (benzo[a]anthracene, benzo[b]fluoranthene, benzo[a]pyrene, and chrysene). OSHA analyzed 110 samples, the majority of which did not contain PAHs. However, eight samples taken on the pile at Ground Zero (averaging 0.4 mg/m³) were in excess of OSHA's PEL for coal tar pitch volatiles of 0.2 mg/m³ (NIOSH, 2002; OSHA, 2002).

Exposure Monitoring from Municipal Fires. Studies of firefighter exposures demonstrate that significant respiratory hazards are present in the smoke and gases from active and smoldering fires. Bolstad-Johnson et al. (2000) monitored firefighter exposures at 25 structure fires and found concentrations of the following:

- acrolein, carbon monoxide, formaldehyde, and glutaraldehyde above the American Conference of Governmental Industrial Hygienists (ACGIH) ceiling values
- benzene, nitrous oxide, and sulfur dioxide above NIOSH or ACGIH short-term exposure limits
- PAHs above the NIOSH REL for coal tar pitch volatiles.

Austin et al. (2001) reviewed five studies of firefighter exposures to municipal structural fires. These studies revealed exposures to organic vapors, toxic gases, and particulates above OSHA PELs (see Table 3.4) and suggest that carbon monoxide concentrations around active or smoldering fires can exceed the NIOSH immediately dangerous to life or health (IDLH) value of 1,500 ppm.

Table 3.4
Range of Chemical Concentrations Reported in Smoke from Municipal Structural Fires

Chemical	Range of Measured Concentrations	NIOSH REL (TWA Unless Otherwise Marked)	OSHA PEL (TWA Unless Otherwise Marked)
Acetaldehyde	n.d. –8.1 ppm	Lowest feasible concentration	200 ppm
Acrolein	0.1–15 ppm	0.1 ppm	0.1 ppm
Benzene	n.d.–250 ppm	0.1 ppm	0.1 ppm
Carbon Dioxide	460–75,000 ppm	5,000 ppm	5,000 ppm
Carbon Monoxide	n.d.–15,000 ppm	35 ppm	50 ppm
Formaldehyde	n.d.–8.3 ppm	0.016 ppm	0.75 ppm
Hydrogen Chloride	n.d.–200 ppm	5 ppm (ceiling)	5 ppm (ceiling)
Hydrogen Cyanide	n.d.–75 ppm	4.7 ppm (STEL)	10 ppm
Hydrogen Fluoride	0.2–7 mg/m³	3 ppm	3 ppm
Nitrogen Dioxide	0.02–10 ppm	1 ppm (STEL)	5 ppm (ceiling)
Particulates (total)	4–20,000 mg/m³	No REL	15 mg/m³
Sulfur Dioxide	0.4–41.7 ppm	2 ppm	5 ppm

SOURCE: Austin et al. (2001).
NOTES: ppm = parts per million. STEL = short-term exposure limit.

Defining the Magnitude of Hazardous Exposures

The preceding discussion describes the form, composition, and measurements of potential chemical exposures at a building collapse event. It does not, however, define the level of exposure that can be considered safe for emergency responders. This is a critical issue for assessing inhalation hazards and selecting appropriate respiratory protection.

Respirators are selected so that the calculated maximum-use concentration for any hazardous chemical present is greater than the concentration of that chemical in the ambient air. Maximum-use calculations are calculated as the product of the respiratory equipment's assigned protection factor (APF) and the OSHA PEL for each chemical. Specific values for APFs are established by NIOSH and ANSI for approved respirators (See Table 3.5). There are several exposure benchmarks for determining a chemical's acceptable dose. However, none is universally applicable for all situations. Examples of some of these standards are presented in Table 3.6.

Table 3.5
NIOSH and ANSI APFs for Particulate Exposures

Respiratory Type	APFs	
	NIOSH	ANSI
SCBA[a, b]	10,000	10,000
Powered Air-Purifying Respirator (PAPR)[c, d]	50	1,000
Full-Facepiece APR[d]	50	100
Half-Mask APR[d]	10	10
Disposable Filtering Facepiece Respirator[e]	5	10

SOURCES: ANSI (1992), NIOSH (1987).
NOTES: [a] Refers to device operated in positive-pressure (i.e., continuous-flow or pressure-demand) mode. Operation in demand mode has an APF of 50. [b] ANSI does not assign a protection factor for SCBAs because workplace studies suggest that all users may not achieve an APF of 10,000. However, ANSI suggests that 10,000 be used as the maximum protection factor for an SCBA for emergency planning purposes.
[c] APF applies to PAPR used with full facepiece. [d] APRs only provide chemical protection if appropriate chemical cartridge is used. [e] Disposable filtering facepiece respirators only provide protection from particulate exposures.

Table 3.6
Established Benchmarks for Defining Hazardous Exposures

Organization	Exposure Benchmark	Comments
OSHA	PEL	Not to be exceeded as an 8-hour TWA
	STEL	Not to be exceeded as a 15-minute TWA
	Ceiling value	Never to be exceeded
NIOSH	REL	Not to be exceeded as a 10-hour TWA
	STEL	Not to be exceeded as a 15-minute TWA
	Ceiling value	Never to be exceeded
American Conference of Governmental Industrial Hygienists (ACGIH)	Threshold limit value	Not to be exceeded as an 8-hour TWA
	Short-term exposure limit	Not to be exceeded as a 15-minute TWA
	Ceiling	Never to be exceeded
American Industrial Hygiene Association (AIHA)	Workplace environmental exposure levels (WEELs)	Benchmarks provided with identical definitions to OSHA PELs and ceiling values
	Emergency response planning guidelines (ERPGs)	ERPG-1, ERPG-2, and ERPG-3 are 1-hour exposure benchmarks defined for the levels of severity of effects
Department of Energy	Temporary emergency exposure limits (TEELs)	Defined the same as ERPGs for TEEL-1, TEEL-2, and TEEL-3 with the addition of a no-effect benchmark (TEEL-0)

OSHA is the only organization that publishes enforceable exposure limits. OSHA PELs dictate exposure levels that should not be exceeded as an eight-hour TWA. These are generally set assuming continuous occupational exposures for eight hours per day, five days per week, over a typical individual's career. OSHA short-term exposure limits (STELs) are 15-minute TWA concentrations that are not to be exceeded at any time during a work shift. Finally, OSHA ceiling values refer to concentrations that must never be exceeded.

NIOSH and ACGIH have each developed exposure limits that parallel the OSHA PELs, STELs, and ceiling limits. NIOSH has established RELs that are based on a 10-hour TWA and IDLH values that, as the name implies, "[pose] an immediate threat to life or would interfere with an individual's ability to escape from a dangerous atmosphere" (29 CFR 1910.120(a)(3), 1999, p. 353). Similarly, the ACGIH publishes TWAs, STELs, and ceiling limits for threshold limit values (TLVs) that have similar definitions to the OSHA values. In general, NIOSH and ACGIH values are more conservative exposure limits than are OSHA standards.

OSHA PELs are commonly used as the basis for a respirator's calculated maximum-use concentration because they are the lowest of the OSHA exposure limits. However, OSHA PELs are not always based on exposures with characteristics faced by emergency responders. TWAs, including OSHA PELs, NIOSH RELs, and

ACGIH TLV-TWAs, are generally set based on continuous exposures over a career at a 40-hour-per-week job. In contrast, emergency responders generally face hazardous chemical exposure only for repeated short durations, a few hours at a time, and generally not during every normal-duty shift. In the case of response to multistory-building collapse events, the historical infrequency of these events suggests that local emergency responders may only expect to experience one such event during their careers.

Recognizing that emergencies require special considerations, the American Industrial Hygiene Association (AIHA), the Department of Energy, the Department of Defense, and the EPA have developed exposure benchmarks for emergencies.

The AIHA maintains lists of workplace environmental exposure levels (WEELs) and emergency response planning guidelines (ERPGs). The WEEL definitions parallel definitions for OSHA PELs, STELs, and ceiling limits. On the other hand, ERPGs are intended to inform planning in the event of short exposures to workers and the public from catastrophic releases as opposed to routine operations. Three levels of ERPGs are defined as the maximum airborne concentration below which it is believed that nearly all individuals could be exposed for up to one hour without experiencing (or, in the second two levels, developing) the following:

- ERPG-1: "other than mild transient adverse health effects or perceiving a clearly defined, objectionable odor"
- ERPG-2: "irreversible or other serious health effects or symptoms which could impair an individual's ability to take protective action
- ERPG-3: "life-threatening health effects" (U.S. Department of Energy, "ERPG Definitions and Background Information," undated).

The Department of Energy has developed temporary emergency exposure limits (TEELs). TEELs are defined similarly to ERPGs with the addition of a benchmark for which most individuals experience "no appreciable risk of health effects" (TEEL-0) (U.S. Department of Energy, "Definitions for Different TEEL Levels," undated). On a chemical-by-chemical basis, TEELs are based on NIOSH-, OSHA-, or AIHA-defined benchmarks.

The National Research Council Committee on Toxicology for the Department of Defense has developed emergency exposure guidance levels (EEGLs) to establish concentrations of substances that are acceptable for the performance of specific tasks during emergency conditions lasting less than 24 hours. The greatest limitation of using EEGLs is that they are only defined for 41 substances, some of which are exclusively chemical weapon agents.

Finally, the EPA is developing acute exposure guideline levels (AEGLs) that represent threshold exposure limits for the public and are applicable to emergency exposure periods ranging from 10 minutes to eight hours for prevention of irreversible or life threatening health effects, AEGL-2 and AEGL-3 levels, respectively. In addition, AEGL-1 values are being developed for each of five exposure periods (10 and 30 minutes; one, four, and eight hours) as a threshold to prevent transient and reversible effects. Like EEGLs, the small number of chemicals for which levels have been adopted limits the application AEGLs to environments encountered after a building collapse.

The decision about which benchmark should be used to determine the maximum-use concentration is inherently chemical- and event-specific. Toxicology suggests that some chemicals, such as silica, can cause chronic health effects after only brief exposures to high concentrations. This suggests that the conservatism provided by the OSHA PELs, NIOSH RELs, and ACGIH TLV-TWAs is often prudent.

Biological Hazards

The primary biological hazards potentially present after the collapse of a large building include bloodborne pathogens from infected humans who might be casualties of the collapse and wastewater pathogens from damaged building sewage systems.

Pathogens relevant to biological hazards at a multistory-building collapse event include bacteria, viruses, or fungi. Bacteria are microscopic one-cell organisms; viruses are generally smaller than bacteria but must actually invade human cells to cause disease; and fungi are parasites that generally feed on dead and decaying material but can also infect humans.

Bacteria, viruses, and fungi can be found in and on almost all surfaces and environments. However, there are fewer than several hundred species of known human pathogens, and most of these do not easily infect humans (Mims, 1982).

Infection requires three conditions: (1) a susceptible host, (2) a viable pathogen present in sufficient quantity, and (3) entry into the host. These three conditions are commonly referred to as the chain of infection (Araujo and Andreana, 2002).

The susceptibility of the host can markedly influence infection—including the genetic constitution, status of the immune system, and current health status. Clearly, we do not all suffer from flu when flu season arrives—yet we are all probably exposed. The same is true for more deadly pathogens. For instance, an accidental inoculation of 249 babies with tuberculosis resulted in 76 deaths; however, the remainder survived with no adverse consequences (Mims, 1982).

Pathogens also have what is known as a "minimal infective dose," "disease-producing dose," or "lethal dose." This means that a certain quantity of the agent is needed to cause an infection, disease, or death, respectively. These critical doses vary by pathogen. For example, 10 shigella bacteria are needed to cause dysentery, whereas 100 million cholera bacteria are needed to cause dysentery. These critical levels are subject to some debate because they depend heavily on the host characteristics, the pathogenicity of the pathogen, the environmental conditions, and how one defines an infection or disease (Mims, 1982).

A pathogen's viability in the environment also affects the risk of infection. Some pathogens can survive for an indefinite period in extremely harsh conditions (such as in boiling water). For example, anthrax spores are known to have survived outdoors for more than 70 years (Mims, 1982). However, the majority of pathogens are viable only in limited ranges of temperature, humidity, and pH. Many pathogens are unstable outside a host, and many are destroyed by sunlight (specifically ultraviolet light). This is why humans cannot contract rabies or the plague by touching contaminated surfaces (Mims, 1982). This is also one reason why some pathogens are endemic in some regions and not others.

Finally, transmission of the pathogen must occur. Six generally accepted types of pathogen transmission occur: respiratory, fecal/oral, venereal, vector, vertebrate/reservoir, and vector/vertebrate reservoir. Transmission necessitates contact with bodily fluids, aerosols, mucous membranes, water, food, insects, or animals.

The chain of infection is pertinent for emergency responders to a building collapse. First, emergency responders are normal susceptible hosts for pathogens. Second, viable pathogens can be present in sufficient quantity in buildings to cause potential infection. Third, the hazardous air quality, work environment, and response activities present multiple potential routes for entry into the host (e.g., from inhalation of aerosols).

While some pathogens will be present in any building, other less common infectious diseases, and agents at higher concentration, might be present if the building is a hospital or houses a nursing home or microbiology laboratory. Also, all buildings have what is called a microbial ecology (Cole and Cook, 1998). Potential pathogens can be found in fireproofing material, insulation, damp wood, ceiling tiles, air conditioners, and carpets. Isolated cases exist of legionellosis (Legionnaires' disease) and aspergillosis causing problems in buildings, but under usual circumstances, potential pathogens in buildings are generally not problematic. However, in a building collapse, pathogens in building materials could be released in aerosols. In addition, with a building collapse, sewage can be released, and blood from victims may be present. Therefore, in the following sections, we describe the potential pathogenic hazards emergency responders may face from typical waterborne pathogens, from bloodborne pathogens, and from aerosols.

Waterborne Pathogens

Waterborne pathogens are organisms transmitted through direct contact with water sources that are most often contaminated with human feces or sewage. Although urine can contain pathogens (e.g., venereal pathogens), transmission of these pathogens in water is minimal. This is because pathogens found in urine are highly sensitive to conditions outside the body and quickly become inert (Feachem, 1983).

Waterborne pathogens can be transmitted through ingestion, inhalation, or skin absorption. For example, transmission may result from drinking contaminated water or touching one's mouth (when eating or smoking) after getting sewage contamination on the hands, breathing aerosolized contaminants, or wading in raw sewage. The vast majority of these pathogens are transmitted through ingestion, but it is important to note that some pathogens can enter the body through intact skin (e.g., leptospirosis) or damaged skin (e.g., tetanus).

The waterborne pathogens are more diverse than bloodborne pathogens and include numerous enteric bacteria,[4] viruses, parasites, and fungi. Sewage treatment plant workers and sewage maintenance workers are in contact with waterborne hazards and thus are potentially chronically exposed to pathogenic microorganisms. One study identified sewage workers as having a higher frequency of headache, dizziness, sore throat, skin irritation, and diarrhea (Scarlett-Krantz et al., 1987). Similarly, a retrospective study identified wastewater treatment workers as having a higher prevalence of gastroenteritis, gastrointestinal symptoms, and headaches (Khuder et al., 1998). Thus, some evidence exists that these workers probably exhibit elevated infection rates from some pathogens. Researchers have debated whether this is really the case. Moreover, other studies have not identified an association between these workers and more serious conditions such as hepatitis, enteric pathogens, and cancer (Clark et al., 1984; Lafleur and Vena, 1991; Trout et al., 2000).

Some important points should be noted. First, most waterborne pathogens are not fatal in healthy hosts. Most cause symptoms akin to food poisoning; thus, they can incapacitate a response team, and enforcement of good hygiene and proper food and water sources is necessary. Second, the prevalence of these pathogens in the United States is low. Thus, the risk of infection is small even if emergency responders are directly exposed to the sewage (e.g., through piercing of boots). In addition, prevention of infection from wastewater pathogens is relatively easy and includes using proper hygiene and wearing protective clothing.

In general, waterborne pathogens pose little risk to emergency responders, since the chance of exposure to waterborne pathogens is small. Given adequate protection and low levels of exposure, it is unlikely that emergency responders will become infected from a waterborne pathogen.

Bloodborne Pathogens

Bloodborne pathogens are transmissible only when blood or other body fluids from an infected person (living or dead) enter a person not immune but susceptible. Contact with bloodborne pathogens (from persons or surfaces) is not sufficient to cause an infection. These pathogens must enter the body through mucous membranes

---

[4] "Enteric" is a general term given to bacteria that inhabit the intestines.

(e.g., eye, nose, mouth) or the skin via an open wound, scrape, or rash. While the risk of transmission is relatively low—due to the low number of people in the general population who are infected and the requirement for actual exchange of sufficient inoculum of blood or other bodily fluids—it is still possible, and contact with blood and bodily fluids should be avoided.

The three bloodborne pathogens of greatest concern are all viruses: HIV, hepatitis B virus (HBV), and hepatitis C virus (HCV) (NIOSH, undated). Cures do not exist, and treatment is very limited for each of these pathogens. The prevalence in the general population of HIV is 0.4 percent, HBV 5 percent, and HCV 1.8 percent (CDC, 1999, 2005). These are low prevalence rates, but at a collapse site with 1,000 injuries or deaths, for example, 72 cases of these bloodborne pathogens would be expected if the prevalence rates for the general population apply.

Even after exposure to these pathogens, the risk of infection in each case is low. For HBV, the likelihood of infection from a single needle stick contaminated with blood from a patient infected with HBV ranges from 6 to 30 percent; for HCV it is 1.8 percent; and for HIV, 0.3 percent (CDC, 2005).

Although the overall risks to emergency responders at a multistory-building collapse are small, we should be careful not to underestimate these potential risks for transmission to emergency responders when treating victims or handling human remains. Emergency responders are also at risk of cuts and scrapes from numerous sharp objects (e.g., broken glass, exposed rebar). These cuts can provide an exposure route if responders are in contact with infected victims or human remains.

In summary, it is unlikely, but possible, that an emergency responder will be exposed to contaminated blood after a building collapse. This hazard is greatest when responders are helping victims or handling human remains. Even if exposure to these pathogens occurs, the risk of infection in each case is low. However, because these pathogens are life threatening, precautions are prudent when emergency responders are involved in high-risk activities.

Airborne Pathogens

Many microorganisms are able to exist in aerosols of less than 5 microns in diameter, which is the size range required to enter the respiratory system (Owens, Ensor, and Sparks, 1992). Fungal spores range in size from 2 to 5 microns; bacteria from 0.3 to 10 microns; and viruses from 0.02 to 0.30 microns (Cole and Cook, 1998).

Aerosols can also persist for long periods. Cases exist in which airborne infections have been transmitted one hour after the source of the aerosol was gone (Bloch et al., 1985). In other cases, particles can become resuspended through disturbance and activity in the vicinity. Thus, emergency responders could be at risk from pathogens contained in aerosols.

Infectious diseases that can be contracted from aerosol contact include tuber-culosis, influenza, measles, chickenpox, psittacosis, legionellosis, meningitis, pertussis, and aspergillosis.

Some diseases can be contracted from airborne bacteria and fungi that were part of the microbial ecology of the collapsed building. For example, aspergillosis can come from fireproofing, Legionnaires' disease from air conditioners, and staphylo-coccus infections from ventilation systems.

Workers exposed to fungal spores can develop diseases. For example allergic al-veolitis can develop (also know as farmers' lung, bagassosis, bird fanciers' lung, sube-rosis, malt workers' lung, mushroom workers' lung, and maple bark-strippers' lung). However, in most cases, this is a hypersensitivity pneumonitis requiring repeated ex-posure.

In an emergency response situation, water is also likely to be present—either from extinguishing fires or from broken water lines. This exacerbates growth of mold and fungi (Kuhn and Ghannoum, 2003). Materials such as wood, jute, wallpaper, and cardboard are particularly vulnerable to mold and fungi growth (Gravesen et al., 1999). In a warm, moist environment, molds can grow rapidly in a matter of days.

Exposure monitoring data do not provide estimates of the concentrations of airborne pathogens that could be present at a building collapse site. However, preva-lence of aerosol-transmitted diseases, building microbial ecology literature, and the potential for water to be present at a collapse site suggest that emergency responders will be exposed to some airborne pathogens, particularly molds and fungi.

Atypical Exposure to Water-, Air-, or Bloodborne Pathogens

The preceding sections describe the normal exposure routes for pathogens. However, at a structural collapse, atypical pathogen exposures can also occur. For example, aerosolization presents a theoretical exposure route for bloodborne and waterborne pathogens. Similarly, bloodborne pathogens can theoretically be transferred through contact with contaminated water. The feasibility of each of these atypical exposure routes is discussed below.

Bloodborne Pathogens in Aerosols. In a building collapse, bloodborne patho-gens might be released in an aerosol. Much research has addressed the question of transmission of viruses and aerosol exposure for trauma surgeons and dentists. Trauma surgeons and dentists create aerosols when using power tools and could risk transmission of bloodborne infections by way of aerosols. As a recent article stated, "there are no epidemiologic or laboratory studies documenting the transmission of bloodborne virus by way of aerosols" (Cole and Cook, 1998, p. 453).

Bloodborne Pathogens in Water. Several studies have examined the ability of bloodborne pathogens, particularly HIV, to survive in water and wastewater. HIV has been shown not to be shed in feces or urine of infected persons (Gover, 1993). Thus, it is unlikely to be found in water or wastewater (Riggs, 1989). As Moore states, "no recovery of infectious HIV from any environmental water source has been reported" (Moore, 1993, p. 1437). HBV and HCV are also sensitive to environmental conditions: They are able to survive in the environment, but their ability to do so is thought to be limited (Sattar et al., 2001).

Waterborne Pathogens in Aerosols. There appears to be considerable debate concerning the transmission of sewage-borne pathogens by way of aerosols (Wright, 2002). Several deaths may have resulted from sewage-borne pathogens (staphylococcus aureus) by way of sludge aerosols ("Researchers Link Increased Risk of Illness to Sewage Sludge Used as Fertilizer," 2002). The National Research Council of the National Academy of Sciences concluded that there may be public health risks from using sewage as a commercial fertilizer sprayed onto farmland ("Researchers Link Increased Risk of Illness to Sewage Sludge Used as Fertilizer," 2002). Research has also shown that enteric bacteria are viable in aerosols, and 88 percent of them are less than 4.7 microns in diameter and therefore capable of causing infection via inhalation (Laitinen et al., 1994).

As stated previously, with a few exceptions, most water- or sewage-borne pathogens are not lethal (in normal hosts). However, this is based on usual fecal-oral route of transmission. Infection following aerosol exposure to sewage may result in infections of atypical sites, such as the respiratory tract. Pathogens in atypical sites often cause more serious problems than they would otherwise (Mims, 1982).

Although the literature on sewage pathogens in aerosols is incomplete, it would seem prudent to protect emergency responders from these potential risks. However, we should note that the risk of sewage becoming aerosolized is probably small because of the location and small quantity of sewage typically retained in a typical multistory commercial or residential building.

Concluding Remarks

The preceding discussions provide an overview of the multiple hazards emergency responders encounter at a multistory-building collapse event. The character and magnitude of the combined hazard is dependent on the activities undertaken and location within the response site. The structural collapse and response activities create multiple physical hazards throughout the disaster site including electrical hazards, excessive noise, vehicle and heavy equipment traffic, sharp objects, falling, and falling object hazards.

Every building collapse will be different in terms of the building's size, building materials used, hazardous materials that may be stored by tenants, and the presence and duration of fires after the collapse. Thus, the limited data available make it difficult to have clear estimates of how high chemical exposures could be. However, a few general conclusions can be drawn based on what data are available. Building collapse and smoke from fires create serious respiratory exposures. Around fires, these exposures can include hazardous levels of VOCs, PAHs, chlorinated hydrocarbons, carbon monoxide, and other common combustion by-products. Hazardous levels of asbestos, silica, SVFs, or simply total particulate matter may also be present whether there are fires at the site or not.

Situations in which biological hazards are high are well defined at a building collapse event. Literature on aerosol transmission of pathogens indicates that only molds present a significant respiratory risk at a building collapse. Bloodborne pathogens, such as HIV, HBV, and HCV, present risks only in the event of direct contact with infected bodily fluids. At a collapse event, this could occur whenever responders are treating victims or handling human remains. As stated previously, the chain of infection makes risks from other infectious diseases or waterborne pathogens unlikely. Situations where these hazards are high, such as pooled sewage, are easily identifiable, and the diseases are generally completely treatable with only minor, temporary effects.

CHAPTER FOUR

Emergency Response to Structural Collapses

The hazards emergency responders face at a structural collapse are determined by the activities they engage in and their location at the event. The personnel involved in a structural collapse response will be highly dependent on the type of event. In general, eight categories of personnel will be involved in most responses to a large structural collapse:

- firefighters
- law enforcement officers
- EMS responders
- USAR or technical rescue personnel
- emergency managers
- skilled support personnel, including construction, trade services, utility, transit, public works, and other private-sector workers
- employees of federal, state, and local response support, public health, or other agencies
- volunteers, both organized and independent.[1]

For example, approximately 5,130 individuals were working at the WTC collapse site on a daily basis (Elisburg and Moran, 2001). Of these, there were about 1,200 firefighters; 2,000 police officers; 496 USAR team members; and 1,350 construction workers.

Even a partial structural collapse requires a significant emergency response effort. While the number of personnel involved in a response operation will be dependent upon the surface area to search and the number and extent of any fires, the number of emergency responders available in the city may also influence the mix of personnel available to participate. The complexity and intensity of such an operation presents logistical challenges to the distribution of PPE and supplies. Particularly in

---

[1] Independent volunteers, those not connected with a specific organization managing their involvement in response operations, are also called convergent volunteers.

the early phases of operations, emergency responders will have to rely largely on what they bring with them or what prior planning makes readily available.

The following sections describe the hazard environment faced by responders at a structural collapse, their typical response activities, and the PPE ensembles currently used by most emergency responders.

Defining the Hazard Environment

At a structural collapse scene, the hazard environment faced by emergency responders will not be uniform across the entire site. In areas very close to the collapse scene, the levels of hazard will be significantly higher than those further removed from the immediate vicinity. To describe the variation in hazards across such an incident scene, the adoption of terms generally applied to different areas at a hazardous materials response operation is highly recommended. Under EPA designations, a hazardous materials scene can be divided into three areas: the exclusion zone, the contamination reduction zone, and the support zone. These areas are also commonly referred to as the hot, warm, and cold zones, terms that we will use from here forward (Hawley, 2000, p. 115). As described below, the terms *hot, warm,* and *cold* can easily be adapted to the response to a collapsed building and serve to identify the severity of hazards present.

The hot zone is the area closest to the collapse, where direct hazard control (e.g., firefighting, stabilizing structures, controlling chemical spills) and victim search and rescue must be carried out.[2] The hot zone is defined specifically to identify the areas of highest hazard. At a structural collapse, the hot zone is characterized by potential exposure to falling objects, unstable work surfaces, electricity, respirable dust particles, fires, and blood from casualties of the collapse. Because this is the area where responders are in the most danger, it is the zone in which they require the most protection.

Surrounding the hot zone, the warm zone is established to provide an area to control access to the immediate disaster site, manage direct response operations, and carry out activities such as responder and equipment decontamination. This zone is characterized by reduced physical hazards; respirable dust particles, chemical hazards, and blood from casualties of the collapse may also be present.

Outside the warm zone, the cold zone is defined for activities not directly involved in rescue activities and to manage traffic into and out of the response operation. The cold zone is established so that responders working in this area are not exposed to hazards. The outer boundary of the cold zone is the incident perimeter. The

---

[2] Depending on the specifics of an incident, a single collapse scene might have multiple hot zones with different types of hazards and operational requirements.

size and number of collapsed buildings, number of victims, and the cause and extent of the building collapse determine the perimeters of the hot and warm zones. In routine hazardous materials operations, the perimeter of the zones and the activities that occur in the zones are generally well defined. For example, the hot zone would be defined to encompass the materials or areas that pose significant risk to responders and only workers directly involved in hazard mitigation would be present. In contrast, at a building collapse event, it is more difficult to make a clear distinction about what activities would occur in the hot, warm, and cold zones. For example, in the aftermath of the WTC collapse, the dust cloud covered a significant portion of lower Manhattan (Jackson, Peterson et al., 2002). Imposing the hazmat response zones at a multistory-building collapse event will likely create large hot and warm zones with many types of responders working across zones. Thus, responder PPE demands depend both on what activities in which they are involved and on where the activities are conducted on the site.

Response Activities at a Structural Collapse

Several phases and operations occur in a structural collapse. For example, the Phoenix Fire Department (PFD, 2004) identifies five distinct phases of response:

- phase 1: arrival on scene
- phase 2: prerescue operations
- phase 3: rescue operations
- phase 4: selected debris removal
- phase 5: debris removal and termination.

Arrival on the scene is concerned with command and coordination functions. Carrying out these functions requires establishing a chain of command, positioning equipment, and setting up a staging area from which operations can be managed. Prerescue operations involve assessing possible hazards at the site. At the same time, the incident command establishes a perimeter and, in coordination with the police, maintains access into and out of the site. During rescue operations, command implements an action plan to search for remaining victims. If the location of victims is unknown or if victims are potentially buried, then debris must be removed. Finally, general debris removal begins when it has been ascertained that no live victims remain at the site.

Work at a building collapse can be extremely demanding physically. The combination of hazards that particular responders face depends on their roles during the response and the zones in which those roles must be carried out.

Response in the Hot Zone

Immediately following the collapse, a spontaneous response will occur. This will involve uniformed responders present in the area, uninjured victims of the collapse, and observers who happen to be near the event. Until incident command is established at the response, this spontaneous effort will put all participants at risk of injury or death, as they will not have appropriate PPE. As soon as possible, incident command should establish control of the collapse scene and response activities.

Because the hot zone contains the collapse scene itself, it represents the central focus of response and rescue activities. As a result, fire department personnel will almost certainly be working in the hot zone. Prerescue operations, among the first organized emergency response tasks, are undertaken to assess possible hazards present at the collapse site. Emergency rescue requires locating and removing victims from the collapse site. Hazard mitigation involves reducing hazards in the area and preventing any other possible hazards from contaminating the area. These activities require working in a rubble- and debris-filled environment, possibly in the presence of fires and airborne chemical hazards. Firefighters may also need to assist injured victims or handle human remains.

For structural collapses within the United States, it is likely that USAR or technical rescue personnel will arrive at the site within several hours after the collapse. For major collapse incidents, additional USAR teams would likely arrive within days. These teams would also be involved in emergency rescue and extrication within the exclusion zone. Collapse rescue operations generally involve digging, tunneling, cutting, and selective removal of debris. This type of work exposes these personnel to physical, chemical, and biological hazards similar to, if not greater than, those encountered by fire department personnel.

EMS personnel are likely to be in and around the hot zone assisting emergency rescue efforts. However, because standard EMS tasks involve treating victims rather than searching for them, their hazard exposure may be somewhat different. Their direct contact with patients will likely result in higher exposure to biological hazards, specifically bloodborne pathogens from infected victims.

Electric utility, communications, construction, and trade service personnel are likely to be in and around the hot zone and directly involved in or assisting other responders in rescue efforts. They may, for example, be cutting rebar or concrete, using heavy construction equipment to move rubble, reducing exposure to other risks by shutting down utility infrastructure such as natural-gas supply or electrical power, assisting in transport of people or material at the scene, and acting to restore the functioning of infrastructure systems affected by the collapse. These tasks may be required as early as phase 3 of rescue operations. This will necessitate that these skilled support workers be protected from physical and chemical hazards.

If the collapse is being investigated as a crime scene, law enforcement will also enter the hot zone to collect evidence. Searching through rubble, debris, and human remains for forensic evidence will expose these responders to all the hazards present in the hot zone.

Response in the Warm Zone

The warm zone represents the boundary between the most intense hazards of the incident and the more managed and lower risk environment of the support zone. As a result, victims, material, and responders from the collapse site itself will pass through this zone on their way into or out of the scene. In treating victims rescued from the collapse area, emergency medical responders will likely operate extensively in this zone. Similarly, because of the need for sufficient proximity to maintain awareness of response operations, response managers from a range of organizations may need to operate in this zone.

Members of all the response organizations involved in rescue operations will also operate in this zone, carrying out management roles and tasks such as decontamination of responders, victims, and material from the collapse scene. If the building collapse is believed to be a result of a criminal or terrorist act, law enforcement investigators may need access to both the warm zone and the hot zone in order to collect or preserve evidence. In the event that criminals or terrorists could potentially be present in the vicinity, officers will need to take positions appropriate to protect the public and emergency responders on the scene of the collapse, as well as to apprehend suspected parties.

Finally, as discussed below, logistics, support, and perimeter control activities typically occur in the cold zone. However, the scale and location of a collapse event may demand that these activities be conducted within the warm zone. This will expose groups of law enforcement, volunteers, and utility workers to hazards in the warm zone.

Response in the Cold Zone

Because it is defined by the perimeter of the incident scene where there are no risks from the collapse event, the cold zone contains the logistical and other supporting resources needed to sustain response operations. All responders involved in collapse operations will spend at least part of their time in the cold zone. In their activities controlling the scene perimeter, maintaining security, and managing traffic patterns around the site, many law enforcement responders will spend a significant amount of time there. A significant portion of disaster management activities, such as logistical or interagency coordination performed by emergency managers and state or federal response agency employees, will likely occur in the support zone (although such roles might require activities within the more hazardous inner zones as well). Other responders involved in supporting operations will be located in this zone. For example, many volunteers' activities, such as serving food for responders or managing supplies, will take place in the cold zone.

Emergency Responders' Typical PPE Ensembles

Each of the different groups of emergency responders identified previously faces a unique set of hazards as part of its typical duties. For many, responding to structural collapses—let alone multistory-building collapse events—may be a rare event. Standard PPE made available to responders is most likely determined by the responders' usual activities.

The National Fire Protection Association has developed consensus standards for the design and performance of PPE ensembles associated with specific response activities. Three of these standards are especially relevant for the responders identified previously:

- *NFPA 1951, Standard on Protective Ensemble for USAR Operations* (NFPA, 2001a)
- *NFPA 1971, Standard on Protective Ensemble for Structural Fire Fighting* (NFPA, 2000a)
- *NFPA 1999: Protective Clothing for Emergency Medical Operations* (NFPA, 1992).

These standards provide general guidance that is relevant to many duties and activities the responders at a multistory-building collapse will likely face. Other NFPA standards have been developed for specific operations:

- *Standard on Protective Ensemble for Proximity Fire Fighting* (also known as NFPA 1976) (NFPA, 2000b)
- *NFPA 1977, Standard on Protective Clothing and Equipment for Wildland Fire Fighting* (NFPA, 2005a)
- *NFPA 1991: Standard on Vapor-Protective Ensembles for Hazardous Materials Emergencies* (NFPA, 2005b)
- *NFPA 1994, Standard on Protective Ensembles for Chemical/Biological Terrorism Incidents* (NFPA, 2001b).

Standards in this second group define protective ensembles that provide high levels of protection for conditions that would not be typically expected at multistory-building collapse events. For example, NFPA 1976 ensembles are most often used for fighting fires on ships or around airplane crashes and are not available to most firefighters (NFPA, 2000b).

The sections below describe the equipment that is typical for members of the different response communities. This information provides a foundation for considering what additional or different PPE is required during response to a multistory-building collapse.

Fire Department Personnel

Firefighters are likely to arrive at a structural collapse with PPE that meets the NFPA 1971 standard (NFPA, 2000a). Design standards in NFPA 1971 address garment, helmet, glove, footwear, and interfaces for hoods, wristlets, and eye or face protection. Performance guidelines in these standards cover dexterity, visibility, and the electrical, flame, heat, impact, puncture, abrasion, and liquid and viral penetration protection characteristics of the ensemble components. Respiratory protection for firefighters, though not covered by NFPA 1971, is generally provided by a self-contained breathing apparatus (SCBA). Gloves, boots, and garments are required to provide one hour of viral penetration resistance. The key characteristic of this ensemble is its ability to protect emergency responders from thermal hazards and other physical hazards (e.g., tears and cuts). This causes the equipment to be heavy, warm, and in the case of gloves, reduces the wearers' grip strength and dexterity.

Law Enforcement

Typical PPE worn by law enforcement officers includes shoes, uniforms, a ballistic vest, and possibly a helmet and gloves. Additional PPE is available for special operations, including forced entry and apprehension, bomb disposal, hostage and barricade situations, and crowd control. These ensembles, however, do not protect against the physical and chemical hazards present at a structural collapse. Law enforcement officers do not typically work around collapse structures, chemical hazards, or heavy equipment.

As part of improving the ability to respond to terrorist threats, a limited number of law enforcement departments have purchased air-purifying respirators (APRs) and have provided appropriate training for using this equipment. Additionally, officers are often equipped with latex or nitrile gloves that provide an impermeable barrier to viruses and other pathogens. However, such gloves are not sufficiently durable for working in the rubble associated with a building collapse.

Unlike the fire service, there are no standards that define the design and operational requirements for an overall law enforcement PPE ensemble. Consequently, the degree of protection offered by uniforms will vary among departments.

Emergency Medical Services

Typical EMS PPE ensembles are defined by the NFPA 1999 standard (NFPA, 1992). The EMS standards are focused on protection against exposure to bloodborne pathogens encountered when treating victims or handling human remains. During conventional operations, EMS personnel do not encounter severe physical or chemical hazards. Thus, NFPA 1999 addresses garment, gloves, and face-wear protection from liquid pathogens, providing only minimal protection from physical hazards.[3] EMS personnel are often members of other uniformed response organizations. In these cases, they may have access to firefighting or USAR ensembles and may be prepared to encounter more severe physical and chemical hazards during response.

Urban Search and Rescue

USAR personnel at a structural collapse will include local responders, special units of fire departments, and federal USAR teams. This means that there could be great variety in the PPE that USAR personnel have available to them.

The most appropriate PPE ensemble for USAR work is that specified by *NFPA 1951: Standard on Protective Ensemble for USAR Operations* (NFPA, 2001a). These standards establish PPE requirements to reduce the safety and health risks from hazards encountered during search, rescue, extrication, treatment, recovery, and site stabilization at building collapses. Design standards in NFPA 1951 address garment, helmet, glove, footwear, and eye or face protection. Performance guidelines in these standards cover dexterity, visibility, and the electrical, flame, heat, impact, puncture, abrasion, and liquid and viral penetration protection characteristics of the ensemble components.

USAR teams often work in extended response operations, and the relevant standards reflect this. Performance guidelines are similar to NFPA 1971 (NFPA, 2000a), although equipment is typically lighter, since protection from extreme heat is not provided. Though respiratory protection is not covered by NFPA 1951 (NFPA, 2001a), federal USAR teams are provided half-mask APRs. Gloves, boots, and garments are required to provide viral penetration resistance. The key characteristics of the USAR ensemble is the ability to protect emergency responders from some physical hazards (e.g., tears and cuts) while providing the agility needed for search-and-rescue work and the comfort for long-duration use.

Emergency Managers

The PPE routinely available to emergency managers will vary from locality to locality based on the standard operating procedures of the area. Managers whose activities are generally away from incident scenes in an emergency operations center may not have PPE readily available if and when they need to go to the incident scene itself; conversely, managers with experience in or drawn from other response organizations such as the fire service or law enforcement could have standard equipment for those disciplines available for use.

---

[3] In contrast to the fire service, where there is broad usage of NFPA-compliant protective equipment, questions have been raised about the availability and use of PPE across the full range of EMS organizations. As a result, although standards exist describing EMS PPE, there reportedly is significant variation in the equipment available from organization to organization (LaTourrette et al., 2003).

Skilled Support Personnel

Because of the diversity of organizations that may provide skilled support personnel to a collapse scene, these individuals will have a wide variety of training, experience, and access to PPE. While there are no standards defining the design and performance requirements for the ensemble for these personnel, some of the PPE components are required to meet certain standards. For example, footwear must pass ANSI Z41-1999 (National Safety Council and American National Standards Institute, 1999). Eyewear must meet the required optical, impact, drop, penetration, and flammability performance outlined in ANSI Z87.1-1989 (American National Standards Institute and National Society of Safety Engineers, 1989). Similarly, head protection must meet standards outlined in ANSI Z89.1–1997 (American National Standards Institute and Industrial Safety Equipment Association, 1997).

Federal, State, and Other Local Agency Personnel

Considerable variability exists in the PPE available to responding employees of other public agencies and organizations. Because policies differ from agency to agency, it is difficult to generalize about the types of protection that will be routinely available to these workers.

Volunteers

Volunteer responders at collapse scenes will typically have access to the least, and least standardized, protective equipment. Volunteers who are connected to specific organizations may have protection options available, but there will likely be variation based on the organizations' missions and experience in similar response operations. Independent volunteers will likely have limited protection, if any at all.

Summary

While the location of emergency responders can vary dramatically depending on the nature of the disaster, some generalizations can be made regarding the zones and the responder activities at a collapse site. Fire department personnel are most likely to be in the hot zone, conducting prerescue, rescue, and hazard containment operations. EMS responders are likely to be in and around the hot zone, assisting emergency rescue efforts. Most police will be at the perimeter of the cold zone, controlling site access, though the scale of the event may often require similar operations in the warm zone. Those investigating the collapse as a potential crime may be within the hot zone. In the event that criminal or terrorist threats continue at the collapse site, police may need to enter the hot zone. Meanwhile, operations and administrative staff who are responsible for the location, direction, and safety of emergency responders are most likely to be in the warm or cold zones (Markus, 2002; Vickery, 2002).

Members of each of the preceding responder groups will have some training and access to PPE. The standard PPE ensembles for each group of responders presented previously are intended to protect against hazards encountered during routine work. This standard equipment may not be suitable for response to a multistory-building collapse, which in contrast is a rare or extreme event. For some responders, the standard ensemble is not protective enough. For others, it may provide overly conservative protection and be incompatible with the demands of the response.

CHAPTER FIVE

Guidelines for Emergency Responders' PPE Ensembles

Ultimately, emergency responders assist in a building collapse event to save lives and protect the public. Protecting these responders and not exposing them to unnecessary hazards are of primary importance to achieving this mission. Many of the hazards that responders face at a building collapse event—such as those from falling objects or unstable surfaces—are the same as those present at more routine emergency response incidents. However, as described in Chapter Three, responders will face other hazards that are unique to tall-building collapse events. Based on this characterization, the guidelines focus on three issues that present unique challenges to the response to a tall-building collapse event.

First, biological hazards present a serious, though very limited and well-defined, threat to responders' health and safety. Second, the largest hazard during the first days of the response may be the inhalation of hazardous materials. Finally, typical PPE ensembles for most responders will require addition, removal, or selection of specific PPE components to ensure adequate, but not overly restrictive, protection.

The precise combination of hazards at a disaster is event-specific. The only means of determining those hazards present—and thus definitively protecting responders—is through hazard monitoring. However, even then, incident commanders will have to make difficult choices with respect to protecting responders. These choices involve balancing hazards from multiple sources, available resources, and the goals of the response mission. Within this context, this chapter presents PPE equipment guidelines, challenges, and health and safety implications of not complying with existing occupational standards.

Protection Required from Biological Hazards

Bloodborne pathogens present the most serious biological hazards at a building collapse, because several are incurable, may result in protracted disability, and may be ultimately fatal. However, exposures to bloodborne pathogens are confined to limited and well-defined scenarios. Hazards only exist from contact with bodily fluids. Hazards from bloodborne pathogens are only present when responders are working around infected victims, human remains, or materials that have come in contact with body fluids.

Responders equipped with NFPA-compliant PPE generally do not require additional protection from bloodborne pathogens. Hazardous exposures to body fluids are, in most cases, readily identifiable, and removal and replacement of any contaminated PPE within one hour provides sufficient protection. In addition, as described in the previous chapter, bloodborne pathogens require body penetration for infection to occur. Therefore, NFPA-compliant PPE will also protect against exposure in cases where body fluids are not readily identifiable. On the other hand, responders who are actively treating victims or working with human remains should take extra precautions. These precautions include using gloves that provide an impenetrable barrier to viral pathogens,[1] and goggles or a faceshield to limit exposure to splashes of blood to the eyes, nose, and mouth. Since viral-impenetrable gloves are typically prone to puncture and tear, they should be used as undergloves (or replaced with more durable gloves) when moving through or handling rubble and debris.

Waterborne pathogens may be present across the site. These pathogens would most likely result from sewage in broken sewer lines surrounding the site or from small amounts of sewage that may have been in the building at the time of collapse. Infection is only a concern if the pathogens are able to enter the body through cuts in the skin or contact with mucous membranes (e.g., the eyes, nose, or mouth). Exposures would result either from responders contacting pools of sewage or contaminated water or from contact with waterborne pathogens in the dust at the collapse site. In the event of the former route of exposure (i.e., pools of sewage or contaminated water), responders would easily identify exposure. When such exposures are known to exist at a site, water-resistant clothing and boots should be worn. When such equipment is not used, responders should promptly remove contaminated equipment, wash exposed areas with soap and water, and acquire replacement or decontaminated PPE before resuming work. The latter exposure route (i.e., pathogens in dust) requires only a skin barrier that minimizes contact with the dust and provides protection from cuts, scrapes, and punctures. In any event, the effects of these biological hazards are easily treated and do not generally result in permanent injury, disability, or death. Inhalation of waterborne pathogens presents a very small risk that should be mitigated by respiratory equipment needed to protect against hazardous chemicals in the air.

Dust at the site may contain molds that can cause respiratory irritation or permanent lung damage. As discussed below, respiratory protection for hazardous chemicals in the air can provide adequate protection from these molds.

---

[1] The glove passes the Biopenetration Test Two in NFPA 1999 (NFPA, 1992). This represents a standard test method for resistance of materials to penetration by bloodborne pathogens.

Protection from Inhalation of Hazardous Materials

Direct monitoring data from previous structural collapses are not available to characterize the magnitude of chemical hazards that might be in the air immediately following the collapse of a multistory building. As discussed in Chapter Three, the most applicable site monitoring data comes from analysis of the WTC collapse sites. Monitoring data revealed air concentrations above typical ambient levels—and in some cases, occupational protection levels—for several chemicals including asbestos, VOCs, dioxins, copper, iron oxide, lead, zinc oxide, cadmium, and PAHs. However, the earliest of these data were collected four days after the collapse, on September 14, after the greatest exposures had dispersed or settled out of the air. The mere fact that monitoring results were elevated above typical ambient levels days after the collapse suggests that chemical hazards in the air were present during the first days when no monitoring took place. Selection of respiratory protection is driven by the concentration of respiratory hazards in a collapse environment. Respirators should have a calculated maximum-use concentration greater than the corresponding chemical concentrations in the ambient air. The only means of ensuring the adequacy of respiratory protection is through exposure monitoring and assessment. However, history shows that quantitative exposure monitoring may not be available during the first hours (or even days) of the response to a multistory-building collapse.

In the absence of exposure monitoring results, knowledge of building materials and contents and proximal cues regarding exposure (e.g., visibility) can provide secondary information about the potential respiratory hazards. The characterization of expected chemical hazards in Chapter Three is guided by monitoring data from building fires and information about common building materials and contents of residential and commercial multistory buildings. This characterization identifies five motivating factors for respiratory protection:

- low oxygen environments caused by chemical releases or fires
- smoke from active and smoldering fires containing organic compounds (e.g., benzene, dioxins, PAHs) and toxic gases (e.g., carbon monoxide, hydrogen cyanide, hydrogen chloride)
- irritant dusts from concrete, glass, and other building materials generated by the collapse or by rescue and response activities
- hazardous dusts containing silica, asbestos, metals, or organic compounds generated by the collapse or by rescue and response activities
- biological hazards, primarily from mold spores aerosolized by the building collapse.

Protection for Oxygen-Deficient Environments

The most acute hazards at a building collapse are associated with low oxygen atmospheres, active or smoldering fires, and extremely low visibility conditions. Low oxygen concentrations typically occur when atmospheric oxygen is displaced by the large release of a gas that is denser than air. For example, responders to the WTC collapse were very concerned that Freon, used as a refrigerant for air conditioning systems, could have been trapped in voids created during the collapse (Claudio, 2001). Low oxygen is of greatest concern when working indoors or in a confined space.

An SCBA is the only respiratory equipment option suitable for oxygen-deficient atmospheres at a multistory-building collapse event. If low oxygen conditions are suspected, or work is to be conducted in a confined space, oxygen levels in the air should be monitored. The four-gas monitors used by firefighting companies (i.e., oxygen, carbon monoxide, lower explosive limit, and hydrogen sulfide) meet this need. Note that OSHA regulations about confined space operations require that workers entering a confined space receive task-specific training and monitor atmospheric oxygen levels (OSHA, 1998b).

Respiratory Protection Around Fires

Given that there are several ignition sources in a multistory building (e.g., electrical lines and furnaces) and multiple fuel sources (e.g., building materials and furnishings, heating fuels, and paper), fires can be expected at most multistory-building collapse events. Literature on exposures from municipal fires suggests that the mix of organic and toxic compounds in smoke from active or smoldering fires can be fatal. Under these conditions, the best respiratory protection is an SCBA.

A full-facepiece APR or powered air-purifying respirator (PAPR) with combined particulate, organic vapor, and acid gas cartridge may provide acceptable protection against the organic vapors and toxic gases present in smoke. Each of these respirators has an assigned protection factor of at least 50. This results in a large reduction of exposures and provides responders with significantly improved protection over wearing lesser or no respiratory PPE.

However, APRs are not suitable for work in oxygen-deficient atmospheres or concentrations that are IDLH, because failure of the mask or chemical cartridge would place a responder's life at risk. In particular, when APRs are worn around fires, responder safety can only be ensured if the air is continuously monitored for oxygen and carbon monoxide levels.

Respiratory Protection from Particulate Matter

The WTC collapse generated a dense dust cloud that created near-zero visibility conditions across lower Manhattan. As discussed in Chapter Three, dust at a multistory-building collapse site may contain concrete, asbestos, silica, organic compounds, and metals. The dust generated at the WTC collapse was a severe respiratory irritant. Based on the constituents of building materials, dust at other collapse sites would have similar irritant properties. This section addresses protection required from dust. Subsequent sections address protection from specific constituents that may be part of this dust (e.g., asbestos or silica).

Hazard monitoring is the only means for ensuring appropriate selection of respiratory protection. In the absence of hazard monitoring, conservative protection (e.g., SCBAs or other supplied air respirators) must be used. When exposure monitoring is available, respirators should be selected such that the respirator's calculated maximum-use concentration is below the ambient air concentration in the disaster environment. The maximum-use concentration must be set to meet both the OSHA PEL for the total (15 mg/m³) and respirable (5 mg/m³) particulates not otherwise regulated (PNOR) fractions. Because of the sampling methods used, PNOR is equivalent to the total particulate matter in the air.

When monitoring data are not available, visibility estimates can provide indication of the order-of-magnitude of particulate concentrations in the air following the collapse of a tall building. As the concentration of particles in the air increases, light extinction (i.e., scattering and absorption) increases and visual range decreases. Equation 1 can be used to calculate the relationship between particulate concentrations and visual range (Horvath and Noll, 1967; National Research Council, 1993).

$$\text{Concentration}\left[\text{mg/m}^3\right] = \frac{\left(3.9 \times 10^3\right)}{\left(\text{visibility}\left[\text{m}\right]\right)\left(\text{extinction coefficient}\left[\text{m}^2\,/\,\text{g}\right]\right)} \quad (5.1)$$

In this equation, the extinction coefficient is the measure of how the suspended particles reduce visibility. This coefficient varies based on particle size and chemical composition. For example, aerosols with high levels of elemental carbon are three times more absorbing than those aerosols with low carbon content such as aerosols dominated by sulfates and nitrates. Fine particles (i.e., aerosols that are less than 2.5 microns in diameter) are much more effective at scattering light than an equal weight of larger particles (Malm, 1999).

In general, the range of light extinction coefficients for fine particle mixtures that would typically be generated through fires is between 3 and 10 square meters per gram (Ensor and Pilat, 1971; Mulholland and Croarkin, 2000). The upper end is associated with carbon aerosols that are very opaque while the lower end is associated with aerosols that are lighter in color and less absorbing.

The relationship between visibility and particulate concentrations is subject to two notable limitations. First, this methodology assumes a constant concentration of dust throughout the line of sight being considered. While acceptable across short distances, this assumption will not be valid across longer distances at a collapse site where local variations in dust may be great because of smoke plumes and dust resuspension caused by responder activity. Second, visibility is only an indicator of the total amount of dust in the air and not of the composition of that dust. Even when total dust concentrations are low, specific components of the dust may be present in hazardous concentrations.

Personal accounts and photographic records of the WTC tragedies suggest that particulate concentrations immediately after the collapse of the towers were in excess of hundreds of milligrams per cubic meter (mg/m^3) (National Center for Environmental Assessment, 2002). Responder and victim reports suggest that the larger particulates settled within a few hours, but that poor visibility conditions persisted for days. In select areas, wind and activity would create visibility conditions of less than 0.25 miles (about two city blocks), corresponding to particulate concentrations greater than 1 mg/m^3 to 3 mg/m^3. Table 5.1 presents a worst-case estimate of particulate concentrations calculated using Equation 5.1 for a range of relevant visibility conditions.

Under very low visibility conditions, responders will be unable to assess existence of other respiratory hazards that could exist as the result of fires or confined spaces. Thus, when response activities require entry into areas where the visibility is less than 30 feet (i.e., particulate concentrations greater than 140 mg/m^3), responders should wear an SCBA. Half-mask APRs, full-facepiece APRs, and PAPRs will clog rapidly at these high particulate concentrations and will not provide adequate protection if responders encounter oxygen-deficient atmospheres or IDLH concentrations.

At the WTC, the dust cloud from the tower collapse engulfed some survivors, including emergency responders who had arrived prior to the collapse. Under these conditions, responders may not be wearing or have time to don respiratory protection. Given the irritant nature of these dusts, individuals exposed without respiratory protection to these high dust concentrations should be immediately removed from the site and provided with medical attention.

Respiratory protection is still required even if fires are not present and visibility is greater than 30 feet. Under these conditions, visibility calculations suggest that air concentrations will be less than approximately 140 mg/m^3. Thus, either a PAPR (APF = 50) or a full-facepiece (APF = 50) or half-mask APR (APF = 10) with a combined particulate, organic vapor, and acid gas cartridge would provide adequate protection from total PNOR. Before using respirators, responders should be trained in respirator use and fit-tested.

Measurement of bulk dust samples from the WTC site suggest that less than 10 percent of the dust generated during the collapse was respirable, i.e., made up of particles less than 10 μm in diameter (Lioy et al., 2002). Thus, if respiratory protection meets the OSHA total PNOR standard of 15 mg/m^3, it may also meet the OSHA respirable dust standard of 5 mg/m^3.

Table 5.1
Calculated Worst-Case Particle Concentrations for Observed Visual Ranges

Visibility	Basis	Particle Concentration (mg/m³)[a]
6 ft	Maximum particulate concentration is roughly 50 times the OSHA PEL for total particulate matter (TPM), 15 mg/m³ (i.e., the protection provided by a full-facepiece respirator).	710
30 ft	Maximum particulate concentration is roughly 10 times the OSHA PEL for TPM (i.e., the protection provided by a half-mask respirator).	140
150 ft	Particulate concentrations are approximately twice the OSHA PEL for TPM.	28

NOTE: [a] Concentration calculated assuming an extinction coefficient of 3 m²/g.

The dusty environment surrounding a multistory-building collapse can present respirator hazards even when dust and smoke are not visible in the air. Given the large amount of dust generated at the WTC and Oklahoma City collapses, it is reasonable to expect that responders in the warm zone will need some respiratory protection. All responders in the warm zone should have access to at least half-mask APRs with combined particulate, organic vapor, and acid gas cartridges (APF = 10). This respirator will provide protection from metal particulates, asbestos, silica, and bacterial and mold particulates. However, it will not provide any protection in low-oxygen or IDLH conditions.

Protection from Pathogens and Chemical Hazards

The preceding guidelines discuss protection against total particulate matter. A full-facepiece APR with a combined particulate, organic vapor, and acid gas cartridge can provide protection against specific chemicals at a collapse site, such as metal particulates, asbestos fibers, organic vapors, and silica. But even when the preceding guidelines are followed, responders may be exposed to hazardous chemicals if specific constituents of particulate matter are at concentrations above a respirator's calculated maximum-use concentration. Thus, depending on a building's contents, structural, and architectural materials, responders may be exposed to hazardous levels of chemicals or pathogens even when protected from total particulate matter. Asbestos and crystalline silica are of particular concern because of their toxicity and prevalence in building materials. As always, exposure monitoring is necessary to ensure proper selection of respiratory PPE in accordance with the NIOSH respirator decision logic. If monitoring data are not available, the only way to ensure that responders are not exposed above the NIOSH RELs or OSHA PELs is by wearing SCBAs. However, SCBAs constrain a responder's ability to conduct critical response functions and impose significant logistical constraints on the response mission. The weight and impedance from wearing an SCBA also put responders at risk of injury or death. Selecting respirators to protect from these exposures is further complicated by uncertainty in the marginal risks from one or two days of exposure at levels above NIOSH RELs.

Chapter Three suggests that, although respiratory protection is always required at multistory-building collapse events, there are many scenarios in which an SCBA is overly conservative. This is because many hazardous chemicals are likely to be present in very low concentrations. Chemicals such as arsenic, beryllium, cadmium, chromium, and lead will be uncommon at a collapse site because of their relatively low quantities of use compared with other building materials. The concentrations of these chemicals will be sufficiently low such that if responders are protected to levels below the OSHA PEL for PNOR (15 milligrams per liter [mg/L]), which is measured using total particulate matter, it is unlikely that they will be exposed to concentrations above the PEL for these chemicals.

Table 5.2 presents the critical concentrations[2] for several chemicals and how they compare with reported concentrations from samples of WTC dust. The first column in this table presents the NIOSH RELs for arsenic, beryllium, cadmium, chromium, and lead—some of the most toxic metals detected in dusts at the World Trade Center site. If the concentration of these metals in dust is below the critical concentrations listed in the second column, then protecting workers to the particulate matter REL ensures protection to these chemicals' RELs. In the case of the World Trade Center dust, data from Lioy et al. (2002) suggest that worker exposure to the metals in Table 5.2 allowed for a safety factor of 7 to 180 when compared to the NIOSH RELs. So, if workers are protected against total particulate levels, they will also be protected against these chemicals.

Table 5.2
Critical Concentration of Chemicals in Dust When Wearing Respiratory Protection Required to Meet the NIOSH Particulate Matter REL

Chemical	NIOSH REL (mg/m^3)	Critical Concentration (%)[a]	Concentration in WTC Dust (%)[b]	Safety Factor[c]
Arsenic	0.002	0.013	0.0003	50
Beryllium	0.0005	0.003	0.0004	9
Cadmium[d]	0.005[d]	0.033[d]	0.0009	40
Chromium	0.5	3.333	0.02	180
Lead	0.050	0.333	0.05	7

NOTES: [a] Ratio of the NIOSH REL for that chemical to the OSHA PEL for particulates not otherwise regulated (PNOR) of 15 mg/m^3. The critical concentration is the percentage of a chemical in a dust below which a responder is not exposed above the chemical's REL if already protected so that exposure to PNOR is below the OSHA PEL. [b] Maximum concentration reported in Lioy et al. (2002). [c] NIOSH REL divided by concentration in WTC dust. [d] Cadmium uses the OSHA PEL of 15 mg/m^3, not the NIOSH REL.

[2] The critical concentration is the percentage of a chemical in a dust below which a responder is not exposed above the chemical's REL if already protected so that exposure to particulates not otherwise regulated (PNOR) is below the OSHA PEL.

Other chemicals are expected to constitute a greater percentage of the dust at a multistory-building collapse. For example, if dust created by a collapse is composed of more than 0.3 percent silica or more than approximately 0.02 percent asbestos,[3] responders could be exposed to concentrations above NIOSH RELs even when protected from the particulate matter REL.

This raises the question of what the consequences are of wearing lesser protection. Simple calculations can provide examples for consideration. Assuming total dust concentrations of 150 mg/m^3 and silica and asbestos concentrations of 5 percent and 1 percent,[4] respectively, wearing a full-facepiece respirator reduces exposures significantly, but not enough. Under these conditions, responders would still be exposed to levels three and ten times the NIOSH RELs for silica and asbestos, respectively. Although a full-facepiece APR does not appear adequate, the health consequences of resulting exposures are not always clear.

For example, the marginal risks from short-duration (two-day) exposures at 10 times a NIOSH REL are unknown. It is clear the risk from a two-day exposure is lower than that from a 30-year exposure. For example, the marginal risk from a two-day exposure to many carcinogens is approximately 4,000 times less than the lifetime risk from a 25-year exposure.[5] Although this quantitative reasoning does not apply for some carcinogenic and many noncarcinogenic risks, such as silicosis from crystalline silica exposures, epidemiology does indicate that risks of such exposures are less as the duration and magnitude of exposures decrease (Rodricks, 1992).

Respirators used to protect against particulates also provide protection against molds and other airborne pathogens. Specifically, APRs with particulate or equivalent filters provide protection against the bacterial and mold pathogens that might be expected at a collapse site. 42 CFR 84–certified respirators are tested based on the most penetrating particle, 0.3 μm. Since most bacteria and mold particles are larger than this, proper use of these APRs is protective from the respiratory biological hazards expected at a multistory-building collapse site.

In summary, monitoring data are required to select respirator PPE properly. Without monitoring data, uncertainties in the magnitude and composition of respiratory exposures at a multistory-building collapse dictate that only SCBAs can ensure that responders are not exposed to levels above NIOSH RELs or OSHA PELs. However, SCBAs are heavy and cumbersome; thus, using them can limit responders' abili-

---

[3] This assumes that 1 fiber/cc = 0.03 mg/m^3 (NRC, 1984).

[4] One hundred fifty milligrams per cubic meter is a total dust concentration of 10 times the OSHA PEL for PNOR. At this concentration, visibility would be about 30 feet and a responder would be protected from PNOR when using a half-mask APR. Percentages of 5 percent and 1 percent for silica and asbestos, respectively, are realistic benchmarks for concentration based on samples of dust taken around the WTC disaster site by Lioy et al. (2002).

[5] Assuming a linear dose-response function and a constant exposure concentration, risk from a two-day exposure equals the 30-year lifetime risk divided by ([{2,080 work hours per year} × 30 years]/16 work hours), or 3,900.

ties to engage in critical lifesaving tasks and may place them at even greater risk of immediate injury or death.

Using either PAPRs or APRs significantly decreases responder exposures. PAPRs provide several benefits over both APRs and SCBAs. Because PAPRs provide a constant supply of air at positive pressure using a battery-powered motor, they are not subject to the same fit-testing requirements, mask fogging difficulties, and breathing hindrances that APRs present. In addition, they are lighter and less cumbersome than SCBAs. On the other hand, PAPRs are more expensive than APRs, require an adequate supply of recharged batteries, and consume more cartridge filters because air is constantly passed through them at a high rate.

Both PAPRs and APRs place responders at some level of marginal risk for the few days during which they are responding to the collapse site. Although current knowledge of the chronic effects of short-term exposures does not provide a basis for quantifying this risk, it does suggest that these short-duration exposures present lower risks than lifetime exposures. In choosing between SCBAs, PAPRs, and APRs when exposure monitoring and assessment are not available, incident commanders must balance the increased burdens SCBAs present on lifesaving missions, risks SCBAs present for responders, and risks responders may face while using PAPRs and APRs. Table 5.3 presents the factors for respirator selection discussed in this section.

Table 5.3
Respiratory Protection at a Multistory-Building Collapse

Hazard	PPE Options	Drivers	Limitations
Low Oxygen Atmosphere[a, b]	SCBA	Fire Oxygen displacement	Heavy, cumbersome, and logistically intensive
Active or Smoldering Fires[a]	SCBA	Organic vapor Acid gases Carbon monoxide	Heavy, cumbersome, and logistically intensive
Visibility < 30 ft[a]	SCBA	Total particulate matter Mold spores Inability to detect hazards	Heavy, cumbersome, and logistically intensive
Visibility > 30 ft but Visible Smoke or Dust Haze[a]	SCBA (or other supplied air) or APR with combined particulate, organic vapor, and acid gas cartridge and an N95 prefilter[c]	Total particulate matter Mold spores	APR not protective in low oxygen or IDLH atmospheres. For APR use, monitoring required for levels above PELs to ensure adequate protection.

NOTES: Refer to Table 5.1 for dust concentrations corresponding to visibility estimates. [a] Expected conditions in hot and warm zones. [b] Greatest concern in confined spaces. [c] Accepted APRs for particulate matter: PAPR, full-facepiece cartridge respirator, or half-mask cartridge respirator with goggles, as required.

Other Limitations of Air-Purifying Respirators

Cartridges used on APRs and PAPRs have limited lifetimes. They must be replaced when the absorbent is exhausted or when the particle filters clog and breathing becomes difficult. At a minimum, respirator cartridges should be replaced once per shift to ensure adequate protection. In the dusty environment following a building collapse, filters will often become clogged before the absorbent is exhausted. N95 prefilters should be used to limit particulate loading to the cartridge and extend the cartridge life.

Implications for Responders' Typical Ensembles

Working under hazardous conditions is normal for emergency responders. Responders' standard PPE ensembles, as described in Chapter Four, are assembled to protect against these hazards. The duration, magnitude, and diversity of exposures described in previous sections, however, create conditions that require modifications to responders' standard PPE ensembles.

In some cases, responders' typical PPE is designed for conditions that are less harsh than what might be expected at a multistory-building collapse event. Additional protection is then required to ensure responder safety, and this protection must be compatibly integrated with the other ensemble components. In other cases, responders' PPE is intended for hazards that are not expected during the response. The additional protection provided can impair responders' ability to maneuver and may even create additional safety hazards.

Required modifications to responders' PPE ensembles are based on the equipment with which responders are typically equipped and the hazards present when they are working. The former has already been reviewed in terms of responders' standard PPE ensembles. The latter depends on where on the disaster site the responder is working.

The following sections describe required modification to PPE ensembles for USAR teams, firefighters, EMS personnel, law enforcement officials, and construction workers, trade personnel, and volunteers working at a multistory-building collapse event. Table 5.4 provides a summary of these modifications.

Table 5.4
PPE Ensembles and Respiratory Protection Required at a Multistory Structural Collapse, by Control Zone

PPE Component	Warm Zone	Hot Zone	
		No Fire	Fire or Low Visibility
Ensemble (garments, gloves, boots, footwear, eye and face protection)	Enhanced USAR[a]	Enhanced USAR[a]	NFPA 1971
Respirator[b]	Half-mask to full-facepiece	Half-mask to SCBA	SCBA

NOTES: Required protection applies to any responder working in the designated zone. Task-specific PPE may also be required (e.g., additional eye or face protection for torch cutting). [a] Enhanced USAR represents NFPA 1951 ensemble (NFPA, 2001a) plus additional biological protection when treating victims or handling human remains and a lighter helmet meeting NFPA 1977 standards (NFPA, 2005a). [b] Respirator designations reflect the range of respiratory protection expected to be required based on hazard characterization in Chapter Three. Additional protection may be necessary as required by site-specific information.

Immediate Responders

Law enforcement will likely be among the first emergency responders to a multistory-building collapse. For example, patrol cars and street officers may be the closest to a building at the time of a collapse event, and some may even be exposed to the initial collapse hazards. Immediately following the event, they will become part of a spontaneous emergency response. This response will also include victims of the collapse who are not incapacitated and witnesses near the incident.

None of these individuals will have the respiratory, head, eye, or skin protection to protect against the hazards expected at a multistory-building collapse. Thus, all those involved in the immediate aftermath of the building collapse require medical evaluation, and possibly medical attention and screening.

Urban Search and Rescue Teams

The USAR ensemble, as specified in NFPA 1951 (NFPA, 2001a), is the most appropriate for response to a multistory-building collapse. USAR teams often work in extended response operations. The mix of hazards that USAR teams are trained for is similar in kind, if not in magnitude, to those expected at a multistory-building collapse event. Thus, the PPE ensemble worn by USAR teams already corresponds to many of the recommendations highlighted in the previous guideline sections.

USAR equipment is typically light and designed for maximum mobility with protection from physical hazards expected around a collapsed structure. Eye and respiratory protection are commonly used for hazards expected in a dusty environment. In some cases, single-use full-body garments can be used to avoid contamination of clothing and PPE. For many of the activities of the response to a multistory-building collapse, all workers should have protection that meets USAR requirements.

The USAR ensemble does not provide significant protection against heat and flames. When fires are present, most likely within the hot zone, a structural fire-fighting (NFPA 1971 [NFPA, 2000a]) ensemble is required. Otherwise, the standard USAR ensemble requires three modifications to address the environment and hazards at a large structural collapse.

First, the USAR ensemble components are rated to provide an impermeable barrier to bloodborne pathogens. However, this barrier is only adequate so long as the gloves and their seams are intact. Since exposures to bloodborne pathogens will be easily detectable, this protection suffices to allow responders to decontaminate or replace PPE following inadvertent exposures. When exposures to bloodborne pathogens are more likely, it is prudent for USAR teams to wear further protection from biological hazards, such as latex or nitrile gloves and a faceshield. Once again, single-use full-body garments can also be used to reduce decontamination requirements. Examples of conditions where bloodborne pathogen protection is necessary include instances when responders are expected to be actively treating victims or handling human remains.

Second, the NFPA 1951 helmet standards currently provide more protection for heat than is needed when fires are not present (NFPA, 2001a). This additional thermal resistance makes the helmets heavy. For example, the average weights of NFPA 1951, NFPA 1971, and NFPA 1977 helmets are approximately 41 oz., 45 oz., and 20 oz., respectively (NFPA, 2002). Responders to the WTC, Pentagon, and Oklahoma City bombing incidents reported that wearing heavy helmets for long periods caused neck stiffness or other discomfort (Jackson, Peterson et al., 2002). In the absence of extreme heat conditions, the additional NFPA 1951 features (NFPA, 2001a) are not required, and lighter NFPA 1977 helmets (NFPA, 2005a) should be used. In fact, the NFPA is considering a revision of the NFPA 1951 standard because of this issue (NFPA, 2002). This and the preceding modification are referred to as "enhanced USAR" in Table 5.4.

Finally, USAR teams do not typically wear respiratory protection beyond half-mask respirators. Hazards at a multistory-building collapse event may require use of more protective respirators such as full-facepiece APRs, PAPRs, or SCBAs. As discussed previously, respirators should be chosen such that the calculated maximum-use concentration is above the contaminant concentration in the ambient environment.

Firefighters

The ensemble for structural firefighting, as outlined in NFPA 1971 (NFPA, 2000a), protects responders from severe hazards working around active fires and intense heat. When fires are present, this ensemble is the only appropriate PPE. Thus, responders may need to wear the NFPA 1971–compliant ensemble in the hot zone following the collapse of a multistory building.

Lessons from the WTC and Oklahoma City events suggest that this level of protection will not be required across the entire site. In fact, the greatest deficiency of the NFPA 1971 ensemble for response to a multistory-building collapse is that it is in many ways too protective. The heat protection incorporated into the NFPA 1971 makes its garments, gloves, and helmet heavy and cumbersome. Wearing this ensemble places responders at greater risk of injury from falls or exhaustion. Furthermore, working among rubble and building debris can cut or otherwise damage this gear.

Firefighters will need alternative clothing and headgear that is lighter and more suitable for response operations that extend beyond a few hours. For conditions when active fires are not present, firefighters need only a PPE ensemble identical to the modified USAR ensemble discussed previously, which incorporates biological protection as necessary.

Firefighters will also need additional respiratory protection and training in how to use this equipment. All firefighters are trained and provided SCBAs. However, there are times at a multistory-building collapse event when an SCBA is inappropriate but respiratory protection is still needed. The preceding section on respiratory protection outlines how APRs may provide adequate protection in many cases at a multistory-building collapse event and are not as physically and logistically cumbersome as SCBAs. Conveniently, many SCBAs are designed to accept APR cartridges when a supplied-air source is not necessary.

Emergency Medical Services

The standard EMS PPE ensemble (NFPA 1999 [NFPA, 1992]) is not intended to provide protection from many of the physical and chemical hazards expected from a multistory-building collapse. Rather, the NFPA 1999 ensemble provides body and face protection from liquid, biological hazards—namely bloodborne pathogens. This level of protection is largely adequate for work in the cold zone, where there are not physical and chemical hazards. However, EMS responders may also need to enter the warm or hot zones.

If EMS personnel are required to work in the warm or hot zones, additional PPE will be required. Since chemical and physical hazards are greater in these zones, EMS personnel will require clothing, gloves, footwear, and head protection equivalent to that worn by the USAR teams. Since EMS staff will most likely be treating victims, gloves and face protection from bloodborne hazards is still necessary. Finally, just like other responders working in the warm and hot zones, EMS personnel will require respiratory protection, as discussed previously.

EMS staff will not generally be working in the presence of active fires. Rescue of victims located in or near active fire zones should be performed by firefighters wearing PPE compliant with NFPA 1971 (NFPA, 2000a). Treatment and evacuation by EMS staff should occur once such victims are moved to safer areas.

Law Enforcement

The primary roles of law enforcement during the initial hours and days of the response are to control the event perimeter and investigate the site as a crime scene. For perimeter control, law enforcement responders should be removed from the physical and chemical hazards at the collapse unless, as discussed in Chapter Four, law enforcement assistance in access control is required in the warm zone.

Additional PPE is necessary if law enforcement responders must enter the warm or hot zone. In this event, law enforcement responders need head, eye, body, foot, hand, and respiratory equipment equivalent to the modified USAR ensemble discussed previously. Since greater respiratory protection is required (a half-mask APR, full-facepiece APR, PAPR, or SCBA), law enforcement personnel who will likely need to enter the warm and hot zones of a building collapse need to be part of a certified respiratory protection program to ensure they have the medical screening and training required to wear appropriate respirators.

Regardless of entry into the hot and warm zones, all law enforcement officials will need viral penetration–resistant (e.g., latex or nitrile) gloves and eye or face protection if they are expected to assist in treating victims from the collapse.

Construction Workers, Trade Personnel, Volunteers, and Other Responders

As previously discussed, many other responders will be involved in a multistory-building collapse event. These include workers from the construction industry, trade industry, and utility companies, as well as volunteers attending to early response activities. While these groups will not often work in proximity of active fires in the hot zones, they will have roles across the rest of the disaster site. Providing PPE for these groups presents a significant challenge because of the variability that exists with respect to the equipment and training each community can be expected to have.

Emergency response planning must consider the need to provide appropriate protection to these groups of responders. In all cases, except respiratory protection, this simply involves maintaining adequate stores of extra equipment consistent with the modified USAR ensemble discussed previously. However, additional planning is required for respiratory equipment.

Construction, trades, and volunteer personnel will require respiratory protection as outlined in Table 5.3. Before using respiratory protection, responders in these groups must be trained and complete a medical evaluation and quantitative or qualitative fit testing. Allowing individuals to wear respirators without appropriate medical screening and training can place them and those around them at risk. For example, responders who do not have adequate lung function to wear a full-facepiece APR could become disoriented or incapacitated during a hazardous situation in the hot zone, endangering themselves and those around them.

If personnel and facilities cannot be made available at the collapse site to provide the necessary training and screening, individuals who have not received it should be assigned duties that do not require the respiratory protection of a tight-fitting respirator.

Summary

The diversity in hazard exposures, responder tasks, and responders' typical PPE ensembles creates challenges for protecting emergency workers. Since some PPE options are considerably cumbersome, overly conservative PPE selection can potentially be as dangerous as selecting inadequately protective PPE. The incident commander must weigh these factors when directing the response to a multistory-building collapse event.

Protecting responders begins with an understanding of what hazards exist at a specific collapse site. Site monitoring is the only means of definitively identifying hazards present at a disaster site. Logistical challenges at such events can force responders into a position of acting on imperfect information. For these situations, the hazard and event characterizations in Chapter Three provide a foundation for disaster planning.

To ensure a responder is adequately protected, it is appropriate to consider each PPE component individually to assess how much protection is required. Stopping at this point, however, can leave responders with protection that is inappropriate for their specific needs. Responders' entire PPE ensemble must be considered with respect to the expected hazards at a multistory-building collapse event.

CHAPTER SIX

Logistics, Use, and Maintenance Issues at a Structural Collapse

Selecting and purchasing appropriate PPE is only one step of ensuring responder safety during the response to a multistory-building collapse. Although this monograph focuses on PPE, site safety management must account for several other factors. For example, the equipment must also be quickly available and be used correctly. All emergency responders need to know where to get PPE, how to don it, what maintenance is required during use, when and how to clean or replace it, and any limitations of the equipment that could place the responder in harm's way. These factors have implications for PPE: (1) supply and logistics, (2) interaction and compatibility, (3) training, and (4) decontamination. Because these issues are related to the effective selection, use, and maintenance of PPE, they are each discussed briefly below.

Table 6.1 presents how these four issues relate to specific PPE components.

Table 6.1
Significant PPE Issues at a Structural Collapse Site

PPE Component	Supply and Logistics	Interaction and Compatibility	Training	Decontamination
Gloves	x			x
Footwear	x			x
Headwear	x	x		x
Body Garments	x			x
Eye and Face Protection	x	x		x
Hearing Protection	x	x	x	x
Respirators	x	x	x	x

Supply and Logistics

In general, the PPE routinely used by emergency responders falls short of the full PPE ensemble appropriate for use at a multistory-building collapse site. For example, EMS personal and law enforcement officials are usually not issued helmets, work gloves, and respirators as part of their standard uniform. Also, during the response, contaminated or damaged PPE will need to be replaced permanently or temporarily, e.g., while being cleaned. Consequently, there will be a high demand for PPE during a response to a large structural collapse.

Logistics issues are straightforward for many types of disposable equipment, such as hearing protection and gloves. These can be purchased inexpensively and stored conveniently. The largest issue is that multiple sizes and types must be available to ensure that all responders are given the most appropriate equipment. However, maintaining a supply of helmets, goggles, boots, full-body garments, and respirators and respirator cartridges can present significant expenses and distribution challenges.

Firefighters may only have NFPA 1971–compliant helmets and would need to be supplied with lighter models. EMS personnel and law enforcement officials may not be issued head protection as part of their standard uniform. Responders will also need replacements for damaged or contaminated headgear. For all these reasons, emergency response planners should make provisions so responders have ready access to additional helmets meeting NFPA 1951 or NFPA 1977 standards (NFPA, 2001a, 2005a).

Some responders will not have the appropriate boots for work at a multistory-building collapse site. For example, the NFPA 1971 rubber bunker boots used by some firefighters are more cumbersome and uncomfortable than USAR (NFPA 1951 [NFPA, 2001a]) or wildland firefighting (NFPA 1977 [NFPA, 2005a]) boots. Wearing such inappropriate footwear can place responders at risk of falls or slips when working in the unstable work environment of a structural collapse. Firefighters at the site may need multiple pairs of boots for different uses, preferably as part of the standard-issued PPE, since boots must typically be broken in.

Single-use coveralls may be a cost-effective option to limit skin exposure and minimize decontamination requirements. However, if this option is used, planning must account for means of acquiring and distributing single-use coveralls at the collapse site. This could be a large logistical challenge, since they can be used by most responders in the hot and warm zones.

Respirators present the greatest supply and logistical challenges at a multistory-building collapse site. As discussed in Chapter Five, many responders will need respiratory protection. Multiple sizes will be required to ensure responders are given equipment that fits properly, and training, medical evaluation, and fit testing will be required for those who have not already received it. In addition, respirators incorporate several consumable components. A long campaign using SCBAs requires facilities for refill and replacement of exhausted air cylinders. PAPRs require replacement batteries. Air-filter cartridges for APRs and PAPRs must be replaced according to the site's cartridge change-out schedule. At a minimum, cartridges should be changed at the beginning of each shift to ensure that responders are protected. Finally, disposable components, such as N95 prefilters, will be needed throughout the response.

To address supply and distribution problems associated with PPE, disaster management plans for metropolitan areas with multistory buildings should include logistical measures required for the rapid distribution of required PPE to emergency responders.

Integration and Compatibility

Since responders will be wearing multiple PPE components, they must each be integrated into the responder's full PPE ensemble. Incompatibilities between components can compromise both PPE performance and a responder's ability to work or maneuver.

Compatibility is a particularly important issue for head, hearing, eye and face protection, and respirators, since all of these components are worn on the head. Similarly, corrective eyewear can interfere with the function of goggles or respirators. Interference between corrective eyewear, eye protection, and respiratory protection can affect the fit and function of each device, reducing the level of protection provided or creating secondary hazards. Use of a full-facepiece respirator solves all problems of integration for eye and respiratory protection. Spectacle mounts or special lenses may be needed when corrective lenses are required. If lesser respiratory protection is desired, safety managers should consider the integration of eye and respiratory components of the PPE ensemble.

Integration issues of respiratory equipment with head and hearing protection also exist. Many helmets and hearing protectors can interfere with the seal on respirators. The only way to ensure compatibility is to test prospective equipment to see how well it functions together.

Training

Many responders at a multistory-building collapse may be using PPE during operations for the first time. Without proper training on the use of PPE, responders can place themselves or others in harm's way. Training is especially significant for hearing and respiratory protection.

A limitation of respiratory and hearing protection devices is that they can be ineffective because of improper fitting. Not all responders to a structural collapse may have adequate training in proper fitting and use of these devices. In such cases, onsite training will be required.

Before wearing a respirator, emergency responders must receive training in the basics of selection and use of the equipment. OSHA requires that this training include the following:

- the opportunity to handle the respirator
- information about checking for proper respirator fit and seal
- time to become accustomed to wearing the respirator in normal air (OSHA, 1998a).

When tight-fitting respirators are used, individuals must also undergo fit testing to ensure the selected respirator provides adequate protection. Fit tests, through OSHA-approved procedures, must be completed for each brand and respirator model that the emergency responder might use.

Most firefighters, many EMS technicians, and limited numbers of law enforcement officials and trades workers are already covered under a respiratory protection program and will have received this training. For firefighters, the training is often limited to SCBA respirators, in which case additional training on the use and maintenance of cartridge-type respirators is needed. Certification of training and fit testing is typically provided as either a wallet card or a sticker on an identification card. Since fit testing is brand-, model-, and size-specific, respirator supply should be coordinated with training procedures for local responders, or even these certified individuals will require fit testing on alternate brands and models. Individuals not covered by a program will also require additional training at the site before donning a respirator or must be given tasks in the cold zone that do not require respiratory protection.

Decontamination

The two primary sources of contamination are (1) dust from fires and structural collapse and (2) bloodborne pathogens from victims and human remains. Decontamination is required to ensure that responders do not carry contamination with them off the site and, in doing so, endanger themselves and those around them.

Table 6.1 indicates that contamination issues are relevant for most of the PPE components used at a multistory-building collapse response. Specific decontamination concerns and approaches depend on whether the issue of blood or dust is being addressed.

Blood

All the NFPA standards discussed previously for PPE provide for at least one hour of viral penetration resistance. However, all PPE should be replaced or cleaned when it becomes noticeably soiled with blood. The decision to replace or clean PPE is likely dependent upon the type of PPE. For example, it may be most cost-efficient to discard some contaminated gloves. Given the expense and difficulty in finding helmets, boots, body-wear, and respirators, these PPE components will need to be decontaminated.

NFPA standards recommend that PPE be cleaned and dried according to the manufacturers' instructions. Further, the NFPA requires that cleaning be performed by an equipment cleaning service able to handle contaminated clothing. For a structural collapse scenario, preplanned arrangements are required with an equipment cleaning service such that rapid turnaround is achieved.

With contamination from blood, emergency responders should avoid attempting to clean their own equipment. This includes soap and water cleaning and the use of alcohol swabs or other solvents. Self-cleaning is problematic in two ways. First, soap and water is a good disinfectant for many but not all pathogens. Even after cleaning, heavily soiled clothing or gloves may still be hazardous. Second, other cleaning agents or solvents, such as bleach or alcohol, may be damaging to some PPE, including helmets, respirators, and eye or face protection.

Dust

At a structural collapse site, the dust may contain chemicals and is generally of an alkaline and irritant nature. Therefore, cleaning of PPE at the end of a shift is recommended to prevent responders from carrying contamination out and away from the collapse site and into less contaminated areas. Single-use coveralls (e.g., Tyvek®[1] suits) may present a cost-effective alternative to decontamination of body garments when the primary concern is protection from dust at the response site. Rather than decontaminating garments, single-use coveralls can be disposed of after they become soiled or after each use. Such single-use suits do, however, present some limitations.

Specifically, the suits do not provide much protection from tears and abrasions. Thus, more protective PPE should also be worn underneath. But even when worn on top of the lighter protective full-body garments that are available (e.g., USAR full-body garments), they could reduce mobility and increase the heat retention around the emergency responder.

---

[1] Tyvek® is a registered trademark of DuPont.

Summary

While the initial focus of PPE needs is often hazard identification and equipment selection, worker safety is not ensured without considering whether individuals are able to obtain, use, maintain, and clean or dispose of equipment properly.

CHAPTER SEVEN

Remaining Challenges for Protecting Emergency Responders at Multistory-Building Collapse Events

The analysis and recommendations in the preceding chapters are based on available data on potential exposures and health effects associated with a post–structural collapse environment. The guidelines derived from these data provide a framework for emergency response planners to manage training, PPE selection, and supply logistics in emergency preparedness efforts. However, it is perhaps just as important that this analysis highlights where the greatest uncertainties exist around protecting emergency responders in post–structural collapse environments.

Perhaps the most significant uncertainties following a multistory-building collapse are the composition and magnitude of the hazards present in the postcollapse environment. This issue is noted several times throughout this monograph. The PPE recommendations in this monograph are based on hazard characterization in Chapter Three. This characterization describes the expected hazards, but acknowledges that the hazards at any specific site can vary widely based on a building's occupants and contents. Nevertheless, this uncertainty is reducible through hazard monitoring efforts. As monitoring and site-specific data become available following a collapse, responders can gain a more precise understanding of what hazards exist. To the extent that appropriate monitoring capabilities are available, disaster planning and management should incorporate the capability for rapid exposure monitoring and hazard assessment to support selection of appropriate PPE.

Other uncertainties, though not specifically mentioned previously, follow closely from the analysis presented in this monograph. Two of these issues are addressed in the following questions:

- What is required to address the logistical and practical demands of putting these protective guidelines into practice?
- Are OSHA PELs and NIOSH RELs appropriate for infrequent, short-duration, multiple-chemical, high-magnitude exposures?

Key aspects of these two questions are discussed in this section.

Planning for PPE Integration and Compatibility

Although the data included in this monograph provide a guide for the protection required in a post–structural collapse environment, the variety of the responders involved in response to the collapse of a large building can complicate putting these guidelines into practice. At large-scale disasters, distribution of PPE will be necessary. While some responders will likely come to a structural collapse scene equipped with all the necessary protective equipment, many responders may not. Others may come with some PPE, but an incomplete ensemble compared with what is required for full protection. If these responders are to participate in the response, they will require additional PPE. Other responders may need replacement components but not have access to such supplies from their own organizations. As a result, in order to put these guidelines into practice, important logistical details must be addressed.

Disaster planners can address integration and compatibility problems through efficient logistics systems. Purchasing and prepositioning equipment stores, as well as planning for equipment transportation, is required at several levels. This includes consideration both of local stores maintained by large cities and of shared stores maintained by regional jurisdictions or the federal government.

Research into equipment function and usability could spawn technological solutions to integration and compatibility problems that ease logistical constraints. Lighter and more compact equipment, or thinner and stronger materials, would reduce many of the integration and compatibility issues raised at the WTC and Oklahoma City disasters.

Finally, standardization of equipment could also ease integration and compatibility issues. Standards on equipment interfaces, such as respirator cartridge threads, would ease problems with replacement parts. Standards on equipment sizes and designs could ease problems with interfaces between components, such as gloves and clothing or helmets and respirators.

Setting Safe Exposure Limits

Both the levels of hazardous chemical exposures and the levels of exposures that are believed to be safe drive selection of PPE, especially respirators. Levels of hazardous chemical exposures can be determined by monitoring the air, dust, and water around a collapse site. But determining what levels are safe requires a better understanding of the health effects of short-duration, high-magnitude, multiple-chemical exposures.

Evidence from the WTC collapses suggests that the most critical factors for determining the health consequences to emergency responders present during the first days of the response were that exposures were one-time, high-magnitude, and to multiple chemicals. Industrial hygiene has developed approaches to address some of these challenges. For example, the ACGIH additive rule (see Sloss et al., 2005) attempts to address the issue of multiple exposures. However, such approaches are still crude. Existing epidemiology and toxicology studies do not provide exposure data that can provide a more precise estimate of the risks or protective exposure limits for this type of intense, short-term exposure to multiple chemicals.

Increased knowledge of these issues would lead to better PPE guidelines and, ultimately, improvements in responder safety. Thus, ongoing research is warranted in fields such as toxicology and epidemiology to study areas identified by the scientific community as tractable and important. In particular, follow-up studies of those exposed at the WTC or other future building collapse events are crucial to understanding the acute and chronic health effects that result from exposure to the collapse environment.

On the other hand, we should not expect that near-term advances in toxicology and epidemiology will provide useful data related to the dose-response relationship for short-duration, high-magnitude, multiple-chemical exposures. This reinforces the need for exposure standards that reflect the character of the exposures that emergency responders face at multistory-building collapses.

For many of the responders, exposures at a multistory-building collapse site could represent a once-in-a-lifetime exposure, in terms of both the types of substances and the level of exposure. In contrast, conventional occupational exposure limits used to select appropriate respirators, such as OSHA PELs and NIOSH RELs, are often based on continuous exposures for eight hours per day, five days per week, over a typical career in a controlled environment. In addition, these limits are based on health effects data that may consider only single-chemical exposures, as compared with the mixture of exposures that can be expected following the collapse of a multistory building.

Since available scientific evidence does not provide a sound basis for responders' exposure limits, there is a need for continued consideration of approaches for developing alternative occupational exposure limits at multistory-building collapse disasters. Developing such approaches is important for overall safety management of emergency responders and should be based on deliberations among industrial hygienists, toxicologists, and leaders in the emergency response community. These discussions can identify the tradeoffs involved in using PPE to reduce exposure to hazardous chemicals and the risk of possible injury from wearing heavy or cumbersome PPE.

Concluding Remarks

The potential for multistory-building collapses is an unfortunate reality. Multistory buildings exist in all urban areas across the United States. They are vulnerable to a range of forces that could lead to collapse, including earthquakes, wind damage, terrorism, and accidents.

The guidelines in this document pull together current knowledge about potential hazards responders might face at future multistory-building collapse disasters; important criteria and selection processes for PPE; and lessons from previous disasters about the challenges of providing, maintaining, and supporting (through training) emergency responders' PPE needs in a post–structural collapse environment.

The research problems identified in this section can help disaster managers and planners to better prepare emergency responders for multistory-building collapse events. But these events are only a few of the many that emergency responders face. Similar challenges occur with hurricanes, forest fires, earthquakes, and other large-scale disasters. The guidelines in this document and research recommendations in this section will be most beneficial when integrated into broader disaster management and planning.

Advisory Board Membership and Participants in Project Review Workshops

Membership of Emergency Responder Advisory Board

Captain Rick Bruce, San Francisco Police Department

Captain Robert Dubé, Fairfax County Fire and Rescue

Dario Gonzalez, M.D., F.A.C.E.P., Medical Director, New York City Office of Emergency Management

Barbara McCabe, International Union of Operating Engineers

Chief John Norman, Rescue Operations, Fire Department of New York City

Deputy Chief Michael Shields, Chicago Police Department

Assistant Chief Richard Warford, Los Angeles City Fire Department

Participants in Project Review Workshops

Mohammad Ayub, OSHA

Roland BerryAnn, NIOSH

Janice Bradley, International Safety Equipment Association

Mike Brown, NIOSH

Ronald Burger, CDC

Nadia El Ayouby, NIOSH

John Ferris, OSHA

Caroline Freeman, OSHA

Gus Georgiades, OSHA

Philip Goldsmith, Federal Emergency Management Agency (FEMA)

Sandy Gross, FEMA

Frank Hearl, NIOSH

Chip Hughes, National Institutes of Health (NIH)

Andy Levinson,[1] International Association of Fire Fighters

Herb Linn, NIOSH

Kevin Landkrohn, OSHA

Bruce Lippy, National Institute of Environmental Health Sciences (NIEHS)

Richard Metzler, NIOSH

Kerry Murray, NIEHS

Mike Marshall, OSHA

Jon Szalajda, NIOSH

Rodney Winchel, NIH

Ralph Zumwalde, NIOSH

---

[1] During this study, Mr. Levinson took a position with OSHA and continued to participate in project meetings.

References

29 CFR 1910.120, *Hazardous Waste Operations and Emergency Response*, Washington, D.C.: U.S. Government Printing Office, 1999. Online at http://www.osha.gov/pls/oshaweb/owadisp.show_document?p_table=STANDARDS&p_id=9765 as of December 22, 2005.

42 CFR 84, *Approval of Respiratory Protective Devices*, Washington, D.C.: U.S. Government Printing Office, 1999. Online at http://www.access.gpo.gov/nara/cfr/waisidx_99/42cfr84_99.html as of December 16, 2005.

Abbey, David E., Raoul J. Burchette, Synnøve F. Knutsen, William F. McDonnell, Michael D. Lebowitz, and Paul L. Enright, "Long-Term Particulate and Other Air Pollutants and Lung Function in Nonsmokers," *American Journal of Respiratory and Critical Care Medicine*, Vol. 158, No. 1, 1998, pp. 289–298.

ACGIH. See American Conference of Governmental Industrial Hygienists.

Agency for Toxic Substances and Disease Registry, "ToxFAQsTM for Polychlorinated Biphenyls (PCBs)," 2001. Online at http://www.atsdr.cdc.gov/tfacts17.html as of December 15, 2005.

———, "ToxFAQsTM for Synthetic Vitreous Fibers," 2004. Online at http://www.atsdr.cdc.gov/tfacts161.html as of December 15, 2005.

American Conference of Governmental Industrial Hygienists, *2003 TLVs and BEIs: Threshold Limit Values for Chemical Substances and Physical Agents and Biological Exposure Indices*, Cincinnati, Ohio: American Conference of Governmental Industrial Hygienists, 2003.

American National Standards Institute, *American National Standard for Respiratory Protection*, New York, N.Y.: American National Standards Institute, 1992.

American National Standards Institute, and National Society of Safety Engineers, *American National Standard: Practice for Occupational and Educational Eye and Face Protection*, New York: American National Standards Institute, ANSI Z87.1-1989, 1989.

American National Standards Institute, and Industrial Safety Equipment Association, *American National Standard for Industrial Head Protection*, Arlington, Va.: Industrial Safety Equipment Association, ANSI Z89.1-1997, 1997.

ANSI. See American National Standards Institute.

Araujo, M. W., and S. Andreana, "Risk and Prevention of Transmission of Infectious Diseases in Dentistry," *Quintessence International*, Vol. 33, No. 5, 2002, pp. 376–382.

ATSDR. See Agency for Toxic Substances and Disease Registry.

Austin, C. C., D. Wang, D. J. Ecobichon, and G. Dussault, "Characterization of Volatile Organic Compounds in Smoke at Municipal Structural Fires," *Journal of Toxicology and Environmental Health, Part A*, Vol. 63, No. 6, 2001, pp. 437–458.

Axelson, A., and R. P. Hamernick, "Acute Acoustic Trauma," *Acta Oto-Laryngologica*, Vol. 104, 1987, pp. 225–233.

Berge, Bjørn, and Filip Henley, *The Ecology of Building Materials*, Oxford and Boston: Architectural Press, 2000.

Bloch, A. B., W. A. Orenstein, W. M. Ewing, W. H. Spain, G. F. Mallison, K. L. Herrmann, and A. R. Hinman, "Measles Outbreak in a Pediatric Practice: Airborne Transmission in an Office Setting," *Pediatrics*, Vol. 75, No. 4, 1985, pp. 676–683.

Bolstad-Johnson, Dawn M., Jefferey L. Burgess, Clifton D. Crutchfield, Steve Storment, Richard Gerkin, and Jeffrey R. Wilson, "Characterization of Firefighter Exposures During Fire Overhaul," *American Industrial Hygiene Association Journal*, Vol. 61, No. 5, 2000, pp. 636–641.

CDC. See Centers for Disease Control and Prevention.

Centers for Disease Control and Prevention, "Guidelines for National Human Immunodeficiency Virus Case Surveillance, Including Monitoring Human Immunodeficiency Virus Infection and Acquired Immunodeficiency Syndrome," *Morbidity and Mortality Weekly Report*, Vol. 48, No. RR-13, 1999, pp. 1–31. Online at http://www.cdc.gov/mmwr/PDF/rr/rr4813.pdf as of December 14, 2005.

———, "Injuries and Illnesses Among New York City Fire Department Rescue Workers After Responding to the World Trade Center Attacks," *Morbidity and Mortality Weekly Report*, Vol. 51, No. MM0, 2002a, pp. 1–5. Online at http://www.cdc.gov/mmwr/preview/mmwrhtml/mm51SPa1.htm as of December 14, 2005.

———, "Rapid Assessment of Injuries Among Survivors of the Terrorist Attack on the World Trade Center—New York City, September 2001," *Morbidity and Mortality Weekly Report*, Vol. 51, No. 1, 2002b, pp. 1–5. Online at http://www.cdc.gov/mmwr/PDF/wk/mm5101.pdf as of December 14, 2005.

———, "Use of Respiratory Protection Among Responders at the World Trade Center Site—New York City, September 2001," *Morbidity and Mortality Weekly Report*, Vol. 51, No. MM0, 2002c, pp. 6–8. Online at http://www.cdc.gov/mmwr/preview/mmwrhtml/mm51SPa2.htm as of December 14, 2005.

———, "National Health and Nutrition Examination Survey," 2005. Online at http://www.cdc.gov/nchs/nhanes.htm as of December 14, 2005.

Clark, C. S., C. C. Linnemann, J. G. Clark, and P. S. Gartside, "Enteric Parasites in Workers Occupationally Exposed to Sewage," *Journal of Occupational Medicine*, Vol. 26, No. 4, 1984, pp. 273–275.

Claudio, Luz, "Environmental Aftermath," *Environmental Health Perspectives*, Vol. 109, No. 11, 2001, pp. A528–A536. Online at http://ehp.niehs.nih.gov/docs/2001/109-11/EHP109pa528PDF.PDF as of December 19, 2005.

Cole, Eugene C., and Carl E. Cook, "Characterization of Infectious Aerosols in Health Care Facilities: An Aid to Effective Engineering Controls and Preventive Strategies," *American Journal of Infection Control*, Vol. 26, No. 4, 1998, pp. 453–464.

Dockery, Douglas W., C. Arden Pope III, Xiping Xu, John D. Spengler, James H. Ware, Martha E. Fay, Benjamin G. Ferris, Jr., and Frank E. Speizer, "An Association Between Air Pollution and Mortality in Six U.S. Cities," *The New England Journal of Medicine*, Vol. 329, No. 24, 1993, pp. 1753–1759.

Eager, T. W., and C. Musso, "Why Did the World Trade Center Collapse? Science, Engineering, and Speculation," *Journal of the Minerals, Metals, and Materials Society*, Vol. 53, No. 12, 2001, pp. 8–11.

Elisburg, D., and J. Moran, *National Institute of Environmental Health Sciences (NIEHS) Worker Education and Training Program (WETP) Response to the World Trade Center (WTC) Disaster: Initial WETP Grantee Response and Preliminary Assessment of Training Needs*, Washington, D.C.: National Clearinghouse for Worker Safety and Health Training, 2001. Online at http://www.wetp.org/wetp/public/hasl_get_blob.cfm?ID=331 as of December 19, 2005.

Ensor, D. S., and M. J. Pilat, "Calculation of Smoke Plume Opacity from Particulate Air Pollutant Properties," *Journal of the Air Pollution Control Association*, Vol. 12, No. 8, 1971, pp. 496–501.

EPA. See U.S. Environmental Protection Agency.

Feachem, Richard G., *Sanitation and Disease: Health Aspects of Excreta and Waste Management*, Chichester and New York: Wiley for the World Bank, 1983.

Fechter, Laurence D., Guang-Di Chen, and David L. Johnson, "Potentiation of Noise-Induced Hearing Loss by Low Concentrations of Hydrogen Cyanide in Rats," *Toxicological Sciences*, Vol. 66, No. 1, 2002, pp. 131–138.

Fechter, Laurence D., John S. Young, and Lynn Carlisle, "Potentiation of Noise Induced Threshold Shifts and Hair Cell Loss by Carbon Monoxide," *Hearing Research*, Vol. 34, No. 1, 1988, pp. 39–47.

Ford, Larry R., "Reading the Skylines of American Cities," *Geographical Review*, Vol. 82, No. 2, 1992, pp. 180–200.

Gover, N., "HIV in Wastewater Not a Threat," *Water Environmental Technology*, 1993, p. 23.

Gravesen, Suzanne, Peter A. Nielsen, Randi Iversen, and Kristian Fog Nielsen, "Microfungal Contamination of Damp Buildings: Examples of Risk Constructions and Risk Materials," *Environmental Health Perspectives*, Vol. 107, No. S3, 1999, pp. 505–508.

Hanner, P., and A. Axelsson, "Acute Acoustic Trauma: An Emergency Condition," *Scandinavian Audiology*, Vol. 17, No. 1, 1988, pp. 57–63.

Hawley, Chris, *Hazardous Materials Response and Operations*, Albany, N.Y.: Delmar Thomson Learning, 2000.

Hirschkorn, Phil, "9/11 Victims' Names Posted at Ground Zero," CNN.com, September 10, 2002. Online at www.cnn.com/2002/US/09/10/ar911.wtc.names.numbers/index. html as of December 14, 2005.

Hornbostel, Caleb, *Construction Materials: Types, Uses, and Applications*, New York: Wiley, 1991.

Horvath, H., and K. Noll, "The Relationship Between Atmospheric Light Scatter Co-Efficient for Studies of Visibility and Pollution," *Atmospheric Environment*, Vol. 1, 1967, p. 469.

Jackson, Brian A., John C. Baker, M. Susan Ridgely, James T. Bartis, and Herbert I. Linn, *Protecting Emergency Responders, Volume 3: Safety Management in Disaster and Terrorism Response*, Santa Monica, Calif.: RAND Corporation, MG-170-NIOSH, 2004. Online at http://www.rand.org/publications/MG/MG170 as of December 14, 2005.

Jackson, Brian A., D. J. Peterson, James T. Bartis, Tom LaTourrette, Irene T. Brahmakulam, Ari Houser, and Jerry M. Sollinger, *Protecting Emergency Responders: Lessons Learned from Terrorist Attacks*, Santa Monica, Calif.: RAND Corporation, CF-176-OSTP, 2002. Online at http://www.rand.org/publications/CF/CF176 as of December 14, 2005.

Khuder, Sadik A., Tammy Arthur, Michael S. Bisesi, and Eric A. Schaub, "Prevalence of Infectious Diseases and Associated Symptoms in Wastewater Treatment Workers," *American Journal of Industrial Medicine*, Vol. 33, No. 6, 1998, pp. 571–577.

Kuhn, D. M., and M. A. Ghannoum, "Indoor Mold, Toxigenic Fungi, and Stachybotrys Chartarum: Infectious Disease Perspective," *Clinical Microbiological Reviews*, Vol. 16, No. 1, 2003, pp. 144–172.

Lafleur, J., and J. E. Vena, "Retrospective Cohort Mortality Study of Cancer Among Sewage Plant Workers," *American Journal of Industrial Medicine*, Vol. 19, No. 1, 1991, pp. 75–86.

Laitinen, Sirpa, Juhani Kangas, Marjut Kotimaa, Jyrki Liesivuori, Pertti J. Martikainen, Aino Nevalainen, Riitta Sarantila, and Kaj Husman, "Workers' Exposure to Airborne Bacteria and Endotoxins at Industrial Wastewater Treatment Plants," *American Industrial Hygiene Association Journal*, Vol. 55, No. 11, 1994, pp. 1055–1060.

LaTourrette, Tom, D. J. Peterson, James T. Bartis, Brian A. Jackson, and Ari Houser, *Protecting Emergency Responders, Volume 2: Community Views of Safety and Health Risks and Personal Protection Needs*, Santa Monica, Calif.: RAND Corporation, MR-1646-NIOSH, 2003. Online at http://www.rand.org/publications/MR/MR1646 as of December 14, 2005.

Levine, M. S., and E. P. Radford, "Occupational Exposure to Cyanide in Baltimore Fire Fighters," *Journal of Occupational Medicine*, Vol. 20, No. 1, 1978, pp. 53–56.

Lioy, Paul J., and Michael Gochfeld, "Lessons Learned on Environmental, Occupational, and Residential Exposures from the Attack on the World Trade Center," *American Journal of Industrial Medicine*, Vol. 42, No. 6, 2002, pp. 560–565.

Lioy, Paul J., Clifford P. Weisel, James R. Millette, Steven Eisenreich, Daniel Vallero, John Offenberg, Brian Buckley, Barbara Turpin, Mianhua Zhong, Mitchell D. Cohen, Colette Prophete, Ill Yang, Robert Stiles, Glen Chee, Willie Johnson, Robert Porcja, Shahnaz Alimokhtari, Robert C. Hale, Charles Weschler, and Lung Chi Chen, "Characterization of the Dust/Smoke Aerosol That Settled East of the World Trade Center (WTC) in Lower Manhattan After the Collapse of the WTC 11 September 2001," *Environmental Health Perspectives*, Vol. 110, No. 7, 2002, pp. 703–714.

Lippy, Bruce E., "Safety and Health of Heavy Equipment Operators at Ground Zero," *American Journal of Industrial Medicine*, Vol. 42, No. 6, 2002, pp. 539–542.

Malm, William C., *Introduction to Visibility*, Fort Collins, Colo.: Cooperative Institute for Research in the Atmosphere, NPS Visibility Program, Colorado State University, 1999.

Makens, J., *Understanding Transmission Capacity for Wholesale Electric Power Trade*, U.S. Department of Energy, 1996.

Markus, R., telephone conversation with the authors, November 19, 2002.

McKinsey and Company, *Improving NYPD Emergency Preparedness and Response*, New York: McKinsey and Company, 2002a. Online at http://www.nyc.gov/html/nypd/pdf/nypdemergency.pdf as of December 14, 2005.

———, Increasing FDNY's Preparedness, New York: McKinsey and Company, 2002b. Online at http://www.nyc.gov/html/fdny/html/mck%5Freport/index.html as of December 14, 2005.

Mims, Cedric A., *The Pathogenesis of Infectious Disease*, London and New York: Academic Press, 1982.

Moore, Barbara E., "Survival of Human Immunodeficiency Virus (HIV), HIV-Infected Lymphocytes, and Poliovirus in Water," *Applied and Environmental Microbiology*, Vol. 59, No. 5, 1993, pp. 1437–1443.

Morata, T. C., D. E. Dunn, and W. K. Sieber, "Occupational Exposure to Noise and Ototoxic Organic Solvents," *Archives of Environmental Health*, Vol. 49, No. 5, 1994, pp. 359–366.

Mulholland, George W., and Carroll Croarkin, "Specific Extinction Coefficient of Flame Generated Smoke," *Fire and Materials*, Vol. 24, No. No. 5, 2000, pp. 227–230.

National Center for Environmental Assessment, *Exposure and Human Health Evaluation of Airborne Pollution from the World Trade Center Disaster*, Research Triangle Park, N.C.: National Center for Environmental Assessment, U.S. Environmental Protection Agency, 2002.

National Fire Protection Association, *NFPA 1999: Protective Clothing for Emergency Medical Operations*, Quincy, Mass.: National Fire Protection Association, NFPA 1999, 1992.

————, *NFPA 1971, Standard on Protective Ensemble for Structural Fire Fighting*, Quincy, Mass.: National Fire Protection Association, NFPA 1971, 2000a.

————, *Standard on Protective Ensemble for Proximity Fire Fighting*, Quincy, Mass.: National Fire Protection Association, NFPA 1976, 2000b.

————, *NFPA 1951, Standard on Protective Ensemble for USAR Operations*, Quincy, Mass.: National Fire Protection Association, NFPA 1951, 2001a.

————, *NFPA 1994, Standard on Protective Ensembles for Chemical/Biological Terrorism Incidents*, Quincy, Mass.: National Fire Protection Association, NFPA 1994, 2001b.

————, "Proposed Tentative Amendments to NFPA 1951–2001," *NFPA News,* Vol. 6, No. 5, 2002, pp. 1–2.

————, *NFPA 1977, Standard on Protective Clothing and Equipment for Wildland Fire Fighting*, Quincy, Mass.: National Fire Protection Association, NFPA 1977, 2005a.

————, *NFPA 1991: Standard on Vapor-Protective Ensembles for Hazardous Materials Emergencies*, Quincy, Mass.: National Fire Protection Association, NFPA 1991, 2005b.

National Institute for Occupational Safety and Health, "Bloodborne Infectious Diseases HIV/AIDS, Hepatitis B Virus, and Hepatitis C Virus," undated Web page. Online at http://www.cdc.gov/niosh/topics/bbp as of December 14, 2005.

————, *NIOSH Guide to Industrial Respiratory Protection*, Cincinnati, Ohio: U.S. Department of Health and Human Services, Public Health Service, Centers for Disease Control, National Institute for Occupational Safety and Health, Division of Safety Research, 1987. Online at http://www.cdc.gov/niosh/87-116.html as of December 14, 2005.

————, *Occupational Noise Exposure: Criteria for a Recommended Standard*, Cincinnati, Ohio: U.S. Department of Health and Human Services, Public Health Service, Centers for Disease Control and Prevention, National Institute for Occupational Safety and Health, 1998a. Online at http://www.cdc.gov/niosh/98-126.html as of December 14, 2005.

————, *Worker Deaths by Electrocution: A Summary of NIOSH Surveillance and Investigative Findings*, Cincinnati, Ohio: National Institute for Occupational Safety and Health, 1998b.

————, *Preventing Injuries and Deaths of Fire Fighters Due to Structural Collapse*, Cincinnati, Ohio: National Institute for Occupational Safety and Health, 1999.

————, "Summary Report to the New York City Department of Health: NIOSH Air Sample Results for the World Trade Center Disaster Response," 2002. Online at http://www.cdc.gov/niosh/wtcsampres.html as of December 14, 2005.

National Research Council, *Asbestiform Fibers: Nonoccupational Health Risks*, Washington, D.C.: National Academy Press, 1984.

————, *Protecting Visibility in National Parks and Wilderness Areas*, Washington, D.C.: National Academy Press, 1993.

National Safety Council, and American National Standards Institute, *American National Standard for Personal Protection: Protective Footwear*, Itasca, Ill.: National Safety Council, ANSI Z41-1999, 1999.

NFPA. See National Fire Protection Association.

NIOSH. See National Institute for Occupational Safety and Health.

NRC. See National Research Council.

Occupational Safety and Health Administration, "Confined Space Hazards," undated. Online at http://www.osha.gov/SLTC/smallbusiness/sec12.html as of December 15, 2005.

———, "Occupational Safety and Health Standard 1910.134: Respiratory Protection," 1998a. Online at http://www.osha.gov/pls/oshaweb/owadisp.show_document?p_table=STANDARDS&p_id=12716 as of December 15, 2005.

———, "Occupational Safety and Health Standard 1910.146: Permit-Required Confined Spaces," 1998b. Online at http://www.osha.gov/pls/oshaweb/owadisp.show_document?p_table=STANDARDS&p_id=9797 as of December 15, 2005.

———, "OSHA Sampling Results Summary as of 10/08/2002," 2002. Online at http://www.osha.gov/nyc-disaster/summary.html as of December 15, 2005.

OSHA. See Occupational Safety and Health Administration.

Owens, M. K., D. S. Ensor, and L. E. Sparks, "Airborne Particle Sizes and Sources Found in Indoor Air," *Atmospheric Environment*, Vol. 26A, No. 12, 1992, pp. 2149–2162.

Perry, Robert H., Don W. Green, and James O. Maloney, eds., *Perry's Chemical Engineers' Handbook*, 6th ed., New York: McGraw-Hill, 1984.

PFD. See Phoenix Fire Department.

Phoenix Fire Department, "Phoenix Fire Department Operations Manual, Volume 2," 2004. Online at http://www.ci.phoenix.az.us/FIRE/start_here.html as of December 19, 2005.

Prezant, David J., Michael Weiden, Gisela I. Banauch, Georgeann McGuinness, William N. Rom, Thomas K. Aldrich, and Kerry J. Kelly, "Cough and Bronchial Responsiveness in Firefighters at the World Trade Center Site," *The New England Journal of Medicine*, Vol. 347, No. 11, 2002, pp. 806–815.

Radford, E. P., and E. S. Levine, "Occupational Exposure to Carbon Monoxide in Baltimore Fire Fighters," *Journal of Occupational and Environmental Medicine*, Vol. 18, No. 9, 1976, pp. 628–632.

"Researchers Link Increased Risk of Illness to Sewage Sludge Used as Fertilizer," *ScienceDaily*, July 30, 2002. Online at http://www.sciencedaily.com/releases/2002/07/020730075144.htm as of December 19, 2005.

Riggs, J. L., "AIDS Transmission in Drinking Water: No Threat," *Journal of the American Water Works Association*, Vol. 81, No. 9, 1989, pp. 69–70.

Rodricks, Joseph V., *Calculated Risks: Understanding the Toxicity and Human Health Risks of Chemicals in Our Environment*, Cambridge and New York: Cambridge University Press, 1992.

Rom, William N., *Environmental and Occupational Medicine*, Philadelphia, Pa.: Lippincott-Raven Publishers, 1998.

Samet, Jonathan M., Francesca Dominici, Frank C. Curriero, Ivan Coursac, and Scott L. Zeger, "Fine Particulate Air Pollution and Mortality in 20 U.S. Cities, 1987–1994," *The New England Journal of Medicine*, Vol. 343, No. 24, 2000, pp. 1742–1749.

Sattar, Syed A., Jason Tetro, V. Susan Springthorpe, and Antonio Giulivi, "Preventing the Spread of Hepatitis B and C Viruses: Where Are Germicides Relevant?" *American Journal of Infection Control*, Vol. 29, No. 3, 2001, pp. 187–197.

Scarlett-Krantz, J. M., J. G. Babish, D. Stickland, and D. J. Lisk, "Health Among Municipal Sewage and Water Treatment Workers," *Toxicology and Industrial Health*, Vol. 3, No. 3, 1987, pp. 311–319.

Sloss, Elizabeth M., Nicholas Castle, Gary Cecchine, Renee Labor, Henry H. Willis, and James T. Bartis, *Review of Literature Related to Exposures and Health Effects at Structural Collapse Events*, TR-309-NIOSH, Santa Monica, Calif.: RAND Corporation, 2005. Online at http://www.rand.org/publications/TR/TR309 as of December 14, 2005.

Suter, Alice H., "Construction Noise: Exposure, Effects, and the Potential for Remediation; A Review and Analysis," *American Industrial Hygiene Association Journal*, Vol. 63, No. 6, 2002, pp. 768–789.

Thom, David, *Dave Thom's World Trade Center Report*, September 14, 2001. Online at http://www.tgeneva.com/~davethom as of March 7, 2006.

Treitman, R. D., W. A. Burgess, and A. Gold, "Air Contaminants Encountered by Fire Fighters," *Journal of Occupational and Environmental Hygiene*, Vol. 41, No. 11, 1980, pp. 796–802.

Trout, Douglas, Charles Mueller, Linda Venczel, and Ann Krake, "Evaluation of Occupational Transmission of Hepatitis A Virus Among Wastewater Workers," *Journal of Occupational and Environmental Medicine*, Vol. 42, No. 1, 2000, pp. 83–87.

Tubbs, R. L., "Noise and Hearing Loss in Firefighting," *Occupational Medicine: State of the Art Reviews*, Vol. 10, No. 4, 1995, pp. 843–856.

U.S. Department of Energy, "Definitions for Different TEEL Levels," *Environment, Safety and Health*, undated Web page. Online at http://www.eh.doe.gov/chem_safety/teeldef.html as of December 22, 2005.

———, "ERPG Definitions and Background Information," *Emergency Management Issues*, undated Web page. Online at http://www.orau.gov/emi/scapa/erpgdefinitions.htm as of December 22, 2005.

U.S. Environmental Protection Agency, "EPA Asbestos Materials Bans: Clarification, May 18, 1999," Washington, D.C.: U.S. Environmental Protection Agency, 1999. Online at http://www.epa.gov/asbestos/pubs/asbbans2.pdf as of December 15, 2005.

———, *World Trade Center Disaster Response Air Monitoring Data Summaries*, Washington, D.C.: U.S. Environmental Protection Agency, 2002. Online at http://www.epa.gov/wtc/summaries/datasummaries.pdf as of December 15, 2005.

USGS. See U.S. Geological Survey.

U.S. Geological Survey, *Minerals Yearbook*, Washington, D.C.: U.S. Department of the Interior, 2001. Online at http://minerals.usgs.gov/minerals/pubs/myb.html as of December 14, 2005.

———, *USGS Environmental Studies of the World Trade Center Area, New York City, After September 11, 2001*, Reston, Va.: U.S. Department of the Interior and U.S. Geological Survey, 2002. Online at http://pubs.usgs.gov/fs/fs-0050-02/ as of December 14, 2005.

Vickery, A. D., telephone conversation with the authors, September, 2002.

World Health Organization, *Hazard Prevention and Control in the Work Environment: Airborne Dust: Prevention and Control Exchange (PACE)*, Geneva: Department of Protection of the Human Environment, World Health Organization, 1999.

Wright, Machaelle Small, "Sewage Sludge 'Biosolids': A Health and Environmental Crisis and Scandal," *Perelandra Health Watch*, September 12, 2002. Online at http://www.perelandra-ltd.com/AB1473/webpage.cfm?WebPage_ID=313&DID=8 as of December 19, 2005.

Ylikoski, J., "Acute Acoustic Trauma in Finnish Conscripts: Etiological Factors and Characteristics of Hearing Impairment," *Scandinavian Audiology*, Vol. 18, No. 3, 1989, pp. 161–165.